g demands a

mannerisms,

y and pleasant-

e, its forms distinct

he skill of their designer,

outline; elegant, that is, gracious in line and fluid in form; and above all it must possess unmistakably the quality we call "art"—that something which comes from the spirit the designer puts unconsciously into the body of his work. *Frederic William Goudy*, 1940

A B C D E F G H I J K L M N O P Q R S T U V W X Y Z

Frederic Goudy

Sketch
natural

Latest trademark of V P
designed by F W G in 1912

LU
QU
JGS,
JGS,

R m
ffl' &

14

Hadriano

Point No. **3**

Total Number of Characters **45**

fdry Arrangement   **Sept 7**   19**35**

Set **#1**

Cap H .275 at
14pt .024   **14pt**

Cap H ht pat 1.654 type .128	Cap H set 0.275 type " .0213	th cut		48 ── 14pt
A ✓ 9/9/35	a	1 ✓9/12		â
B ✓ 9/7 35	b	2 ✓		á
C ✓ 9/7	c	3 ✓		à
D ✓ 9/10	d	4 ✓		ä
E ✓ 9/9	e	5 ✓		ã
F ✓ 9/9	f	6 ✓		ê
G ✓ 9/9	g	7 ✓		é
H ✓ 9/9	h	8 ✓		è
I ✓ 9/7 35	i	9 ✓		ë
J ✓ 9/9	j	0 ✓		î
K ✓ 9/10	k	$ ✓9/11		í
L ✓ 9/7 35	l	£		ì
M ✓ 9/10	m	.		ï
N ✓ 9/10	n	..		ô
O ✓ 9/10	o	en		ó
P ✓ 9/9	p	em		ò
Q ✓ 9/11	q	*		ö
R ✓ 9/10	r	†		õ
S ✓ 9/9	s	‡		û
T ✓ 9/10	t	‖		ú
U ✓ 9/11	u	§		ù
V ✓ 9/00	v	¶		ü
W ✓ 9/12	w	[		ç
X ✓ 9/11	x	]		ñ
Y ✓ 9/10	y	(		Ç
Z ✓ 9/11	z	)		
Æ ✓ 9/12	æ	'		
Œ	œ	'		
& ✓ 9/11	ff	'		
?	fi	. ✓9/11		
⑫ ✓ 9/13	fl	, ✓9/11		
;	ffi	— ✓9/11		
:	ffl	,		
		◆ ✓9/11		

8041

Venezia Italic

6/1/25

Point No. .... **Arrangement** .... **Set** ....

Geo. W Jones, London 1925

Total Number of Characters ....

		sw			sw						â
✓✓	A	✓✗		✓	a			1			â
✓	B	✓		✓	b			2			á
✓	C	✓		✓	c			3			à
✓	D	✓		✓	d			4			ä
✓	E	✓		✓	e	✓		5			ã
✗	F	✗		✓ ✗	f			6			ê
✓	G	✓		✓	g			7			é
✓	H	●		✓	h			8			è
✗	I	✗		✓	i			9			ë
✓	J			✓	j			0			î
✓	K			✓	k	✓		$			í
✓	L			✓	l	✗		£			ì
✓	M	✓		✓	m			.			ï
✓	N			✓	n			..			ô
✓	O	✓		✓	o			en —			ó
✓	P	✓		✓	p			em —			ò
✓	Q			✓	q			*			ö
✗	R	✗		✓	r			†			õ
✓	S			✓	s			‡			û
✓	T	✓		✓	t			‖			ú
✓	U			✓	u			§			ù
✓	V	✗		✓	v			¶			ü
✓	W			✓	w			[			ç
✓	X			✓	x			]			ñ
✓	Y			✓	y	✓		(			Ç
✓	Z			✓	z	✓		)			
	Æ				æ			'			31
	Œ				œ			'			31
✓✗	&			✗ ✓	ff			'			9
✓✗	?			✓	fi		✓	.			5
✓✗	!			✓✓	fl		✓	,			79
✓✗	;			✗✓	ffi		✓	-			
✓✗	:			✗	ffl		✓	Λ			
31		9		31		3		8			

8041—9-21-1 M-13

Frederic Goudy

D. J. R. Bruckner

DOCUMENTS OF AMERICAN DESIGN

HARRY N. ABRAMS, INC., PUBLISHERS

NEW YORK

FOR DOCUMENTS OF AMERICAN DESIGN
Project Manager: Samuel N. Antupit
Editor: Sarah Bodine
Designer: John Baxter

FOR HARRY N. ABRAMS, INC.
Editor: Eric Himmel
Graphic Production: Doris Leath Strugatz

Pages 2–3
Printer's mark of the Village Press, 1912

Pages 4–5
Goudy's drawings of Kennerley italic

Pages 6–7
Goudy's work sheets for designing Venezia Italic
and Hadriano typefaces

Page 12
Press proof of Village No. 2

Library of Congress Cataloging-in-Publication Data

Bruckner, D. J. R.
  F. W. Goudy / D. J. R. Bruckner.
    p. cm. — (Masters of American design)
  ISBN 0-8109-1035-7
  1. Goudy, Frederic W. (Frederic William), 1865–1947.
  2. Type and type-founding — United States — History — 20th century. 3.
  Printing — United States — History — 20th century. 4. Type designers — United
  States — Biography. 5. Printers — United States — Biography.
  I. Title. II. Series.
  Z232.G68B78 1990   89–18103
  686.2'092—dc20   CIP
  [B]

Published in 1990 by Harry N. Abrams, Incorporated, New York
A Times Mirror Company

Printed and bound in Japan

CONTENTS

PREFACE AND
ACKNOWLEDGMENTS
13

INTRODUCTION
15

CHAPTER ONE
ONE MASTERWORK
18

CHAPTER TWO
GOUDY APOSTOLIC
27

CHAPTER THREE
THE LIFE AND TIMES OF F.W.G.
41

CHAPTER FOUR
GOUDY OUT OF TYPE
74

CHAPTER FIVE
THE ARTISTIC FRIENDLINESS
OF MACHINES
88

CHAPTER SIX
NINE FACES, MANY FAMILIES
97

CHAPTER SEVEN
RETROSPECTIVE:
WAS HE OR WASN'T HE?
112

CHAPTER EIGHT
THE WHOLE WORKS
117

NOTES
141

INDEX
142

DOCUMENTS OF
AMERICAN DESIGN
144

CREDITS
144

OOOOOOOOOOOOO99999999988888
8888877777777766666666655555555544444444433333333322
2222222111111111111&&&&&&&&&&&&&ZZZZZZZZZZ
YYYYYYYYYYYYYYYYYYYYYYYXXXXXXXX
XXXWWWWWWWWWWWWWWWWWWWWW
XWWWWWWWVVVVVVVVVVVVVVUUUU
WUUUUUUUUUUUUUUUUUUUUTTT
TTTTTTTTTTTTTTTTTTTTTTTTTTTTTTTT
TTTTTTTTTTTTSSSSSSSSSSSSSSSSSSSSSSSSSS
TSSSSSSSSSSSSSSSSSSSSSSSRRRRRRRRRRRR
PPRRRRRRRRRRRRRRRRRRRRRRRRRR
RRRRRRRRQQQQQQQQQQQPPPPPPPPPPPP
RPPPPPPOOOOOOOOOOOOOOOOOOOOOOO
LOOOOOOOOOOOOOOOOOOOOOOOOOO
NNNNNNNNNNNNNNNNNNNNNNNNN
MNNNNNNNNNNNNNNNNNNNNNNNMM
LMMMMMMMMMMMMMMMMMMMMMM
MLLLLLLLLLLLLLLLLLLLLLLLLLLLLLK
MKKKKKKKKKKKKKKJJJJJJJJJJJJJIIIIIIIIIIIIIIIII
IIIIIIIIIIIIIIIIIIIIHHHHHHHHHHHHHH
IHHHHHHHHHHHHHHHHHHHHHGGGG
GGGGGGGGGGGGGGGGGGFFFFFFFFFFFFFFF
FFFFFFFFFFEEEEEEEEEEEEEEEEEEEDD
EEEEEEEEEEEEEEEEEEEEEEEEEEEEEEE
EEEEEEEEDDDDDDDDDDDDDDDDDDDDD
DDDDDDDDDCCCCCCCCCCCCCCCCCCCC
CCCCCCCCCBBBBBBBBBBBBBBBBBBBAAAAA
BBAAAAAAAAAAAAAAAAAAAAAAAAAA
AAAAAAAAAAAAAAAAAAAAAAA

PREFACE AND ACKNOWLEDGMENTS

Among people in design there is an impression that a vast amount of information about Frederic Goudy and his work is available. That is a tribute to the overwhelming impression he made on type design during his life, a kind of lingering memory. In fact, in the more than forty years since he died very little has been written about him. There were a few small books of tributes in the late 1940s and '50s. In the past twenty-five years the portion devoted to him in general books on types has shrunk continuously, and there have been no books about him.

There are many reasons for this neglect, but none of them justify it. The principal one is simply that, from the '50s on, printing changed completely. Goudy designed entirely for hot type printing. He had no objections to the many kinds of offset being developed at the end of his life; in fact he said designers would have to rethink the entire esthetic of type design when those methods became dominant. The development of new technologies has been so rapid that, unfortunately, that rethinking has never been done. In any case, writers about design have been so involved with the new methods that they have all but ignored the previous generations of designers. We are the poorer for that neglect.

It is time to redirect attention not only to Goudy but to the world of extraordinary people in design that surrounded him. This book is meant to be a first step. I have tried to indicate how different design was at the turn of the century when Goudy set out — the very notion that someone could make a profession of book designing was quite new in this country, and Goudy's friend Bruce Rogers, whose work in book design has not been equaled since, was virtually alone in making a profession of that work. The distinction between compositors and printers and designers was very blurred. And no one made a living as a designer of type. The big foundries had employees who designed many faces, usually by simply making small changes in someone else's work, but they were largely printers or mechanical people who did their design work on the side.

The era when Goudy came into printing and design was a much more turbulent one than now in terms of ideas. The many magazines devoted to the printing trades in the last decade of the nineteenth century and the first decade of this one are very exciting, full of controversy and wonder about esthetics and principles of design. The wild growth of a rich school of American design in the early decades of this century deserves long and careful study.

Obviously, the separation technology and fashion have set up between that time and ours means there are some problems in terminology in writing about Goudy. Designers now have a vocabulary unknown to Goudy's contemporaries, and he and his colleagues used some words in ways that are strange to us. In this book I have tried to make clear with descriptions what their terminology meant. This requires a little attention, but not so much that anyone should be distracted from the story or the argument here.

There is an amusing irony in one aspect of this book. It is set in a modern version of a Bodoni typeface. Goudy despised Bodoni's types and might have been indignant at being dressed up in one of them. But the books of the Documents of American Design series share a look, and the same type will be used for all of them. A further twist is that Bodoni was notoriously possessive of his designs; the notion that anyone would modify them was anathema to him. But this computer-generated type makes significant changes, and Goudy, always good humored, might have been delighted at the older master's discomfort.

Chief thanks go to Sarah Bodine, the editor of the book; John Baxter, its designer; and Kenneth Windsor, a designer who was deeply involved in the project until he moved to Israel several years ago. Their interest was as delightful as it was stimulating, and their patience often worked as a prod when conscience would not.

The collections of four libraries were absolutely necessary in the preparation of the book, and special thanks are owed them: William Matheson, chief of the Rare Book and Special Collections Division, Library of Congress, Washington, D.C., with special thanks to Peter van Wingen, Robert R. Shields, and Clark Evans; Francis O. Mattson, curator of rare books, The New York Public Library, and his staff; David Pankow, curator of the Melbert B. Cary Graphic Arts Collection, The Rochester Institute of Technology, New York, and his staff; and Robert Nikirk, librarian, The Grolier Club, New York City, and his staff.

Among the individuals to whom special gratitude is due are Joseph Blumenthal, Horace Hart, Steven Heller, Andrew Hoyem, Herbert Johnson, Alexander Lawson, Abe Lerner, Dr. Robert Leslie, A. Provan, Sidney Shiff, and Dietmar Winkler.

D. J. R. Bruckner

During the last twenty-five years of his life, F. W. Goudy was a famous man. He was a popular speaker who traveled across the country, and the Atlantic, year after year giving talks to students, businessmen, clubs — almost anyone who would listen. His books on lettering and

INTRO-
DUCTION

the alphabet had wide influence. His home became a place of pilgrimage for his followers. He was talked about and interviewed on network radio; a Hollywood studio made a film about him and his work; he was a regular presence in newspapers and magazines — not just those addressed to people in printing, publishing, and advertising but in Sunday supplements, national news magazines, even *The New Yorker* and *Popular Mechanics*. He never made much money, but he did have fame.

Forty years after his death even people in the world of print know little about him, except that his name is attached to many typefaces. And there are strange misapprehensions about him, the oddest being that he was a formidably serious presence. That would have amused Goudy. He was a great raconteur with a large repertory of funny stories, and he enjoyed jokes on himself. He was keenly aware of how different he

was from most of his colleagues in design, and he knew very well how to use his eccentricity to his advantage. He was a thoroughly democratic man, typical of the generation of the Middle West after the Civil War, and in his long battle for order and clarity in the printed word he carried the fight down to printers, compositors, mechanics, and the general public in a way few of his contemporaries did. It is that aspect of his personality, in fact, that drew criticism of him during his life and that continues to inspire derogatory remarks about him now. He was certainly overpraised by his admirers while he was alive, but he has been belittled by opponents with a harshness that is hard to understand and impossible to justify.

Among those who remember him — by now all are people who came to know him only after he was famous — some of the old attitudes persist. Joseph Blumenthal, the printer, who has written a valuable history of printed books, says, "He was a great self-promoter and he was a lot of fun to be with. But he was not the great printer or typographer, and I do not think he was even the greatest American designer of type. You would not put him with Daniel Berkeley

Goudy at the entrance to the Bodleian Library, Oxford, June 21, 1929

Updike in printing or Bruce Rogers in typography. And I think Rogers designed the best American type, Centaur."[1] But Blumenthal has also pointed out that Goudy was the one person in the world of printing who had a great reputation outside that world.[2]

Horace Hart, onetime president of the Lanston Monotype Company, says that "Goudy was surely the great American type designer and one who has few equals anywhere, ever. I don't know how many types he made and I am not sure that matters. He designed eight or ten or even a dozen that are classics. Who else in the history of type has done that?"

Herbert Johnson of the Rochester Institute of Technology (R.I.T.), whose knowledge of Goudy's work is unequaled, says, "Goudy was just too democratic for those Eastern guys who were already setting themselves up as an establishment in this business when Goudy came along. He had too much fun for them." And Alexander Lawson, also of R.I.T., thinks "Goudy's strength was the strength of his personality. He understood where the people of the country were moving, deep down some place, and he made his campaign for ideas a personal one. He achieved a lot because people responded to him personally. That is also the source of the criticism. Goudy was a very strong individual." Dr. Robert Leslie, the heart and soul of the Typophiles organization in New York longer than anyone could remember (he was only about twenty years younger than Goudy yet lived until 1987), thought Goudy's strengths and weaknesses were both exaggerated but said, "He inspired printers and compositors and a lot of people no one paid much attention to, and he gave them some

dignity. He deserves honor for that, as much as for his types. He loved to be honored, too. Why not? He deserves that."

Goudy was an actor who made his start at an age when serious people in professions ought to be already established. He offended the snobbish among his peers by seeking the reward they would never accept — applause. But he used his popularity to change the perceptions of his audience and make it more discriminating. His zeal for good design was infectious, if subversive. One of the legacies of John Ruskin and William Morris, who in the nineteenth century had started the movement that gave rise to the whole modern notion of design, was the idea that good design was the possession of the few who know, and from them it should be passed down to the masses. By the time Goudy began designing, it was thought the standards could come only from dedicated scholars and were to be seen in the best work of private presses or a few university presses.

Goudy was about as theoretical as the metal he worked in. But he understood the crowd and wanted the crowd to know. He did not pretend to talk much about what he never tried to do. But he loved to talk about craftsmanship and its standards, and his teaching was extraordinarily effective. Instinctively he was a cowboy, and he thought every person had a right to make his own mark. His talks and his writing were the old populist cry of the American heartland, and he tended to treat the great masters of type design of the fifteenth and sixteenth centuries as honored and intelligent colleagues, not as unapproachable figures in a pantheon.

He ran his own press, the Village Press, for more than thirty-

five years and his own foundry for fifteen. He designed scores of types for the two largest foundries in the country as well as for his own. He wrote books and pamphlets about type and design and founded a journal of type design that is of great historical importance in the history of American design. And, as Herbert Johnson said, he had a lot of fun doing it all.

It is an irony of history that American students of design today should know so little about Goudy. The dominant influences

Above, top: Goudy examining his matrix cutter/grinder under a microscope
Above, bottom: Goudy on the porch of the old mill at Deepdene that was his shop
Opposite: Goudy's hands drawing letters

now are European, although in type design it is allowable to bow to the British occasionally. The very word modern in design is associated in most people's minds with the triumph here of the Bauhaus influence after World War II. In the year Goudy set up his own private press, in fact, the Bauhaus began. In 1902, the Duke of Sachsen-Weimar-Eisenach invited H. Van de Velde, a painter who had become an architect, to establish a school at Weimar. It was Van de Velde who later made

Walter Gropius the head of that school, which became known as the Bauhaus. When Gropius and his school, ejected from Germany by the Nazis, came to this country in the 1930s, very few people outside architecture knew who they were, and yet they were to have the most profound effect on our entire notion of design, including printing.

The postwar revolution in design, which has made people of the Goudy generation so remote to us, would have seemed fantas-

tic to them. Goudy did know the intellectual father of the Bauhaus group, Peter Behrens, whose ideas inspired them all and who had an immense influence on German design, including typography, in the early years of this century. Behrens's approach was to assume control over everything, from architecture to the design of machines and household goods to typefaces. The designed world was to reflect the thought of a single intellect, whether that was the mind of one man or of a group with ideas in common.

When Goudy saw the work of Behrens and of the Bauhaus in Germany in 1925, he passed over it largely as something a bit alien to us.

Now it is he who is a bit alien. But he should not be. It may not be terribly important to know that it was an American, not Europeans, who dominated type design for a long period in this century. But it is important to know about the history of American design, and in that history Goudy is a large figure.

Goudy designed so many typefaces drawn from so many sources that it is difficult to tease out of them character- 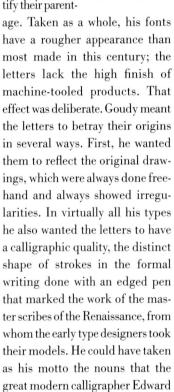 istics that are distinctly Goudyesque. In a sense the variety is a tribute to his imagination and his studies. But in most of Goudy's types one finds traits that identify their parent- age. Taken as a whole, his fonts have a rougher appearance than most made in this century; the letters lack the high finish of machine-tooled products. That effect was deliberate. Goudy meant the letters to betray their origins in several ways. First, he wanted them to reflect the original drawings, which were always done freehand and always showed irregularities. In virtually all his types he also wanted the letters to have a calligraphic quality, the distinct shape of strokes in the formal writing done with an edged pen that marked the work of the master scribes of the Renaissance, from whom the early type designers took their models. He could have taken as his motto the nouns that the great modern calligrapher Edward Johnston of the Royal College of Art cited as the origins of "excellence and beauty" in formal written letters — "sharpness, unity, and freedom" — although Goudy

might have reversed the order. Excepting those types modeled on fraktur, or Gothic, forms, all of Goudy's faces reflected a predilection for the earliest types, especially those of Jenson, and a conviction that Roman inscriptional letters are the finest. And all but the earliest deliberately reveal something of their manufacture; Goudy wanted them to appear to have sprung from the materials and the tools he used and not to imitate characteristics of older methods.

Different designers and printers have their own favorites among the Goudy types. Some great ones have definitely favored Goudy Modern, Goudy Newstyle, and Italian Old Style. I think the type that brings together most characteristics of Goudy types the best and has the most distinctive appearance is Deepdene. It is not as exciting or singular as some others, but it is essential Goudy. Every part of its production was done by his hands, and a study of it will teach the eye what to look for in his other types.

Goudy himself tended to talk about designs in more philosophical terms, and remarks he made in the 1930s about the originality of designs and the intellectual quality of all design bear on judg-

Opposite: Original drawings of Deepdene roman lower case letters
Overleaf: "Deepdene: A New Type," broadside printed at Deepdene, 1927

#54-A

cap line

.730

DEEPDENE : A NEW TY
DETAIL BY THE DESIGN
FIRST OFFERED TO PRI

ETTER-Cutting is a Hand
the Artificers of it, that I*
other ; But every one that
Inclination. Therefore, tho
the general Practice of W
here.... For, indeed, by t
cious Eye may doubt whether they go b
in no Practice whatever, ought to be m

ABOUT OLD-TIME TYPES

THE excerpt above is from the writings
little or no previous type-founding exp
previous experience in any shop, or tutelage

E PRODUCED IN EVERY
ER OF THE FACE · NOW
TERS · SEPT · MCMXXVII

Work hitherto kept ſo conceal'd among
nnot learn anyone hath taught it to any
as uſed it, Learnt it of his own Genuine
gh I cannot [as in other trades] deſcribe
k-men, yet the Rules I follow I ſhall ſhew
appearance of ſome Work done, a judi-
ny Rule at all, though Geometrick Rules,
e nicely or exactly obſerved than in this.

MR. GOUDY'S NEW TYPE

f a type-founder who began operations with
ience. Frederic W. Goudy, likewise without
nder any master, "of his own genuine inclina-

Below: A page from Trattato di scientia d'arme *by Camillo Agrippa, printed by Antonio Blado in Rome in 1553*

ments about all of his work:

I really do believe that I am the first (in this country, at least) to attempt to draw letters for types as things artistic as well as useful, rather than to construct them as a machine might, without regard for any esthetic considerations. I think I must early have developed the idea that type to be successful must create an expression in mass not possessed by another face of similar character; and this difference I have come to consider the essence of "original" type design — not believing that each letter must present some actual and demonstrable difference in outline, or even must exhibit a different set of proportional measurements when compared with other forms of the same letters…. A rather large number of types…are largely the result of pertinacity rather than the evolution of any God-given genius. I like to reason things out and I feel my work is intellectual in that sense.[3]

Deepdene does satisfy the requirement of creating a distinct impression in the mass. It has calligraphic qualities but is free from the overemphasis on scribal characteristics or the shapes of written letters that marks his earlier faces. Two years before he cut Deepdene, Goudy had a matrix-engraving machine made for himself and, once he mastered it, his types changed. In general they became freer. They appear to spring directly from the metal, but they still reveal Goudy's hand. In some he appears to have achieved the dream of Aldus: Deepdene, at least, leaves the impression it was written directly in metal by fiery fingers.

Deepdene does not fall within the standard categories in use in Goudy's day. Certainly it does not fit entirely within the "old style"

or "modern" classifications the old type manuals refer to. In general those terms refer to the very early types on the one hand and those following Bodoni and Didot on the other. Goudy himself said that old style should be angular and modern, round and precise. He noted that the old style types tended to stress curves above the center of the letter as modern did not, and old style had wedged and bracketed serifs, while those of modern types were thin and unbracketed. Those are not very scientific descriptions, but they accurately reflect what most people understood by the terms and they are not unuseful. The present-day student of type will find it even harder to classify Deepdene according to any of the proposed international standards. The one most widely used, first invented by Maximilian Vox in France in 1954 and since modified, has either nine or twelve categories (the "lineale," or sans serif, classification has four distinct parts). In general, it divides the old style into three classes according to such characteristics as the incline of the axis of the curves, the slant of the cross stroke on the lower case e, and the shapes of the serifs. In the Vox list, Didone (a word compounded from Didot and Bodoni) is virtually the old modern unchanged. But there are also such categories as slab serif, glyphic (chiseled rather than calligraphic), script, and graphic (characters suggesting their sources were written rather than drawn). Even Vox suggested placing certain types in several of his categories, and one could distribute letters of Deepdene into half a dozen of them.

At the time Goudy was working on this design he was also drawing five other faces. He said he took a suggestion "for one of

PARTE XXXIII

anco profiteuole, & auantaggioſo il procedere col detto pie ſiniſtro, ponendoſi con quello innanzi, in Prima Guardia, come ne la ſeguente figura, onde ſecondo il parer' mio, et per le ragioni, le quali à tal propoſito giudico eſſer migliori, dico che, ſimili ſorti di Guardie ponno acccttarſi in parte, & con le conditioni giuſtificate, et necceſſarie, che di ſotto ſi diranno, ma non gia, quando cõbatteſſe vno co'l nemico, quale foſſe di pari forza, et ſi ritrouaſſero amendoi in camiſa, e'l detto nemico ſe li preſentaſſe cõtra in detta Guardia di Prima, co'l pie ſiniſtro innanzi, perche fermãdoſi Queſto verſo lui in Quarta ordinaria larga, col pie deſtro innanzi, ſubito giunto, li andarebbe incontro. firmandoſi in Terza ſtretta, et non mouendoſi l'auerſario inſino à tanto, che Queſto ancora foſſe arriuato in detta Terza, ſpingerebbe di Seconda ſopra il ſuo pugnale, cio è de l'auerſario, doue volendo alzarſi la punta con detto pugnale, per mandarla fore con animo di tra paſſar' verſo lui, vei ebbe da ſe à firmarſi la ſpada ne la perſona la quale ne l'approſimarſi, tanto maggiormente anco ſi diſcoprirebbe, & offerirebbcſi al colpo. Il che ſe pure occorreſſe a' Queſto, ritrouandoſi per caſo ne la detta Guardia di Prima, come ſtaua l'altro col pie ſiniſtro innanzi, uolgerebbe alquanto in dentro la ſpalla ſiniſtra, ſolamente per ſchifar il parare, eſſendo prohibito per le ragioni gia dette, accompagnando la ſpada del ne mico in fore, & paſſata via ſe lui ſaltaſſe indietro lo ſeguitarebbe con la punta d'im-broccata deſtra in Quarta larga, & lunga.

I

bdoh

Above and opposite: Deepdene lower case letters

Below: Goudy's favorite broad-side, "The Type Speaks," print-ed in Deepdene italic for a 1933 exhibition in Chicago

I AM TYPE! Of my earliest ancestry neither history nor relics remain. The wedge-shaped symbols impressed in plastic clay by Babylonian builders in the dim past, fore-shadowed me: from them, on through the hieroglyphs of the ancient Egyptians, down to the beautiful manuscript letters of the mediaeval scribes, I was in the making.

With the golden vision of the ingenious Gutenberg, who first applied the principle of casting me in metal, the profound art of printing with movable types was born. Cold, rigid, and implacable I may be, yet the first impress of my face brought the Divine Word to countless thousands.

I bring into the light of day the precious stores of knowl-edge and wisdom long hidden in the grave of ignorance. I coin for you the enchanting tale, the philosopher's moralizing, and the poet's phantasies; I enable you to exchange the irksome hours that come, at times, to every one, for sweet and happy hours with books—golden urns filled with all the manna of the past. In books, I present to you a portion of the eternal mind caught in its progress through the world, stamped in an in-stant, and preserved for eternity. Through me, Socrates and Plato, Chaucer and the Bards, become your faithful friends who ever surround and minister to you. I am the leaden army that conquers the world; I am Type!

FREDERIC W. GOUDY

THIS KEEPSAKE HAS BEEN PRINTED AT AN EXHIBI-
TION SPONSORED BY THE AMERICAN INSTITUTE
OF GRAPHIC ARTS, IN THE MUSEUM OF SCIENCE &
INDUSTRY, OCT. 23 TO NOV. 19, 1933, TO HONOR
THE WORK OF THE VILLAGE PRESS [1903-33].
SET IN DEEPDENE ITALICS, DESIGNED, ENGRAVED
AND COMPOSED BY F. W. G. PRINTED BY HAND ON
ARNOLD UNBLEACHED FROM JAPAN PAPER CO. N. Y.

them" from a Dutch type, which his friend Paul Bennett later identified as Van Krimpen's Lutetia. Walter Tracy, for many years head of the British Monotype Company, has made invaluable comments on seventeen of Goudy's types in his book *Letters of Credit.* He takes the reference to "one of them" to be Deepdene. But Goudy was so vague about which of the de-signs he referred to that identify-ing Lutetia as his model is ex-tremely risky. As Tracy himself says, Deepdene has little similar-ity to Van Krimpen's design. A few of the capitals might be re-lated, but that relationship could come from any number of sources, including other originals that both men had in mind when they were drawing their letters. Lutetia is altogether so much more regular in appearance than Deepdene and of such lighter color that if one takes it to be a model one would have to conclude Goudy deliber-ately set out to violate it, and that is very unlikely.

The Deepdene capitals recall imperial Roman inscriptions more directly than they do any of the Renaissance or later interpreta-tions of those inscriptions, and the lower case letters have the kind of sturdiness one expects to find only in uncials. Deepdene roman has a marked ruggedness, a sim-plicity and directness that set it off from European antecedents in ways not apparent at first glances. It is a very American creation.

The rugged appearance comes in part from Goudy's stress on the vertical. The Deepdene roman vowels are quite round, as one might expect from Goudy — the bowls of the b and d could hardly have been drawn by the older designers — and the o may be the roundest he had made to that time. In fact, Deepdene altogether is

obviously a freehand face, and Goudy's characteristic rounding has disappeared from most of the other lower case letters, especially the m and n, and note the vertical shank of the h. The axis of the curves throughout this face is close to the vertical. That emphasis, along with the deep color of the face, gives it a sturdiness some of Goudy's earlier types lacked. Deepdene does not threaten to roll off the page, but it does have a sense of move-ment; it marches rather than glides.

But, as always with this face, one cannot make a statement that will hold for all letters. The lower case roman a, for instance, has the small bowl and roundness of fifteenth-century faces. The e looks slightly stressed left. The legs of k and r in both lower and upper cases terminate in serifs but have the curve of the pen. And the waist of the k is at an odd height.

William Edwin Rudge, the great printer, wanted to acquire Deep-dene as his own dedicated type. Bruce Rogers was an ardent admirer of it and used the italic for his *Letters from T. E. Shaw.* Goudy never described Deepdene as one of his favorites and it would hardly appear to be a type easily handled by compositors and printers, but printers have long been partial to it. Indeed, through the years Goudy was to design five more Deepdene faces, in addition to the italic, to meet printers' demands — Deep-dene Open Text, Deepdene Text, Deepdene Medium, Deepdene Bold, and Deepdene Bold Italic. At first glance the differences among these faces might make one question giving them a fam-ily name, but in fact there is a closer relationship among them than between any of them and any other Goudy type.

Understandably, Goudy ex-pressed an annoyance with print-

C D G Q

C D G Q

abcde
fghijkl
mnopq
rstuv
wxyz

ers for wanting a bold face of this type. Deepdene has an unusually rich color for a book face, and yet it is far from monochrome. The color comes from his treatment of stems and hairlines on the whole (although it is amusing to notice an attenuation of a few stems that reminds one inevitably of a designer he did not admire — Bodoni). Why the printers needed a bold face is a mystery. Goudy thought the need came from the desire to shock rather than invite readers, and he may have been right. But their desire led him to devising the Bold Italic, which is quite unusual. It is not a deeper version of Deepdene Italic but wholly new. It somehow gets lightness into these weighty letters.

In the Deepdene roman face one ought to notice some characteristics that can be usefully compared with those of Goudy's other types, as well as classic faces.

The capital C, D, and G have the high arches one thinks of as Goudy signatures in his later types. The serifs throughout are unusually flat for Goudy. The tail on the capital Q is vintage Goudy (but compare the tail on the Q in the small capital font). In this face Goudy seems to have taken special delight in illustrating the formation of capital G from C. The variance in width of the capitals should make them a problem in composition, but it doesn't. The capital M is especially interesting. The impression is square, but that comes from the serifs. How does Goudy get the suggestion that the M is splayed, but not much? (A lot of that impression depends on which letters it stands next to.)

The italic is striking. The lower case is for all practical purposes entirely upright; like the first italics, it is really a separate face alto-

Top: Deepdene upper case letters
Left and opposite: Deepdene lower case letters
Above: Goudy at his drawing table

M P T N

M P T N

gether. But is it really? The foot serif of the roman lower case d gives the same pen quality as that in the lower case d italic. The italic lower case g looks like the roman g squashed, even to the point of opening up its tail. The relationships between these two faces is very intriguing. The italic owes a lot to the earliest italics, as well, but a close comparison of it with Aldine italic or Blado will tell one a great deal about Goudy's eye. There are very irritating characteristics in Deepdene italic. The upward pen stroke on the shank of the h is annoying in a way that the same quirk is not in the m and n. Yet when these letters join others in words they come perfectly together and their oddities add to the fluidity and gracefulness of the appearance of words in a type that clearly suggests the writing of a scribe using a reed pen.

Deepdene italic capitals incor-

porate more roman shapes than most italics. The P suggests more of old Roman inscriptions than the roman capital in this face, except that the italic P seems to be bowing. But there are wonderfully uninhibited pen strokes in these capitals, especially in the M, N, and T, that give a page set in the face a lightness and grace without seeming decorative.

That kind of effect in Deepdene, roman and italic, in fact, justifies Goudy's claim that his work was intellectual. The more one plays around with this type, the more one is likely to respect the intelligence of its maker.

Goudy should have kept a journal. We know next to nothing about his day-to-day progress on any given face — except for Kennerley Old Style very early in his career and California Old Style very late. At the time he was making the drawings for Deepdene roman and italic

he was working on six faces, and none of them seems to be influenced by Deepdene or to have any influence on it. How could he draw the 208 characters in these two fonts — 87 roman, 77 italic, 17 small capitals, and 27 swash characters — while he was drawing hundreds of others of very different feeling and keep himself somewhat sane?

In the end the great pleasure of Deepdene is its appearance on the page. By now it has begun to look ageless. It makes a page that has unusual brilliance without looking flashy and one that has solidity without denseness. Andrew Hoyem, who chose it for his beautiful Arion Press edition of the United States Constitution in 1987, said of it: "Deepdene is of the time. It is distinctly American, and classical, and it has dignity. It does not look decorative. It is noble."[4]

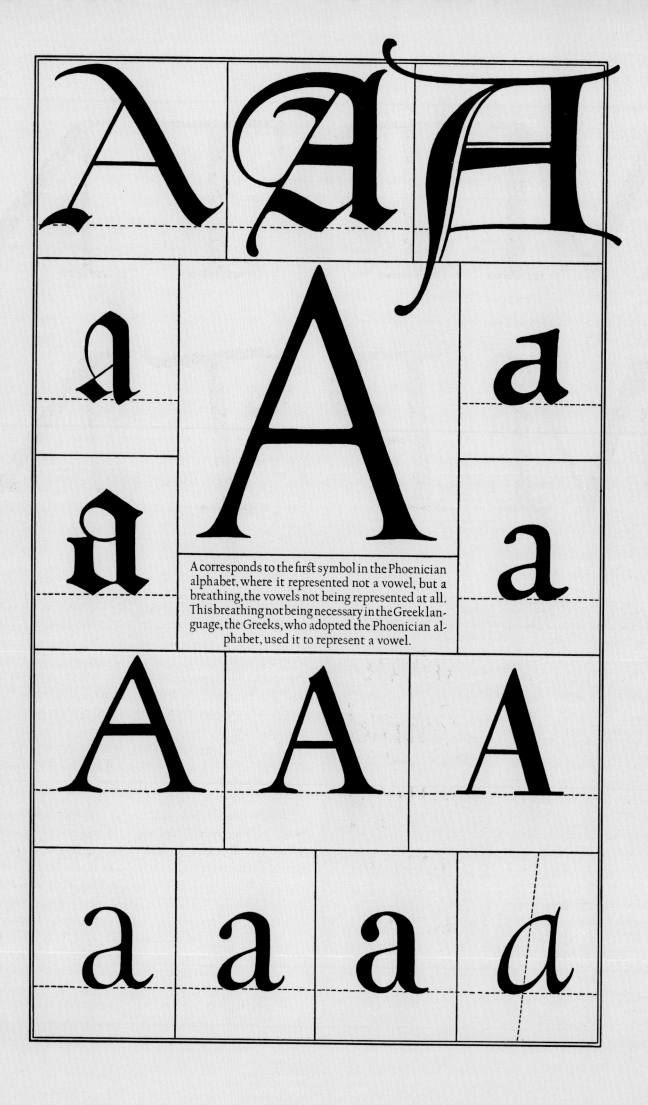

A corresponds to the first symbol in the Phoenician alphabet, where it represented not a vowel, but a breathing, the vowels not being represented at all. This breathing not being necessary in the Greek language, the Greeks, who adopted the Phoenician alphabet, used it to represent a vowel.

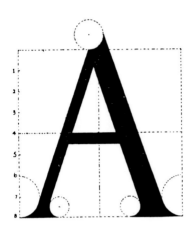

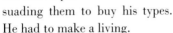

*Left: Goudy's drawings of the
principal forms of the letter A,
from* The Alphabet
*Above: Goudy's illustration of
the construction of roman capitals after drawings by Albrecht
Dürer, from* The Alphabet and
Elements of Lettering

Goudy was a good salesman. When-
ever he started a new enterprise
he issued a brochure appealing to
the good taste of
his customers.
He founded two
journals to ad-
vertise his ideas
about taste.
One, *Ars Typo-
graphica*, he
started with the
clear intention
not only of edu-
cating printers
but also of per-
suading them to buy his types.
He had to make a living.

Some academic critics in design, and some practitioners, are
repelled by that aspect of Goudy's
apostolic career as a teacher —
which is a large part of his conception of himself. Well, even the
best teachers sometimes have mixed
motives. Actually, Goudy's forth-
rightness about the connection between his principles and the way
he made his living is admirable.
For more than thirty years he was
the most listened to and widely
read public spokesman about esthetics in type design and lettering. He was serious, if not original, about his efforts to improve
taste by making people think about
the history of the design of letters, as well as about the standards that should prevail in new
designs and the qualities that give
letters strength and beauty, indi-
vidually and in a line.[5]

Even Stanley Morison, the most

acute and prolific student of type
who objected bitterly to some of
Goudy's claims, said Goudy led
the way in the
United States to
a discussion of
the principles of
good lettering
and type design,
and he acknowl-
edged the pri-
macy of Goudy's
1918 book, *The
Alphabet*, as the
best instructor
available in its
time in the United States. It is
indeed a noble work and one that
designers and students should be
required to know, especially the
chapter titled "The Qualities of
Lettering."

In that book Goudy allowed
only a few pages to a survey of the
history of letters and a description of letters in general before he
announced that his own ideas dif-
fered from, if they did not entirely contradict, those of Leonardo
da Vinci, Albrecht Dürer, Geoffroy
Tory, Joseph Moxon, and a number of lesser authorities of the
Renaissance and the seventeenth
century, and especially from those
of Lucas de Burgo, whose 1494
book on mathematical proportion
virtually dictated the notions those
and other men had about letter
designs for several centuries. At
the time, the authority best known
to readers of English was Moxon,
whose book on letters and types
was published just three centu-

ries ago. In his 1940 book, *Typologia*, Goudy expressed real contempt for Moxon's sloppy vocabulary about type. In *The Alphabet* he had written:

Moxon said of letters that they "were originally invented and contrived to be made and consist of circles, arcs of circles, and straight lines; and therefore those letters that have these figures entire, or else properly mixt, so as the progress of the pen may best admit, may deserve the name of true shape."

But these selfsame curves, arcs of circles, straight lines, also make up letter forms that we do not always consider to be of "true shape"; nor is it possible to entertain the opinion that all letters, although equally composed of these very elements, will necessarily submit to analysis or be reducible to set rules of formation that will make easier the creation of new forms. Such an analysis can, at best, only fix and permit the reproduction of the same form at another time; and even then the quality of life and freedom in the original will be in large part lost in the reproduction. The mere blending together of geometrical elements common to all letter forms, good or bad, is not enough: "true shape" is something more subtle than geometry.

He may have been hitting Mox-

on, but surely his aim was at Leonardo and many other influential Renaissance thinkers.

Goudy's tastes were wholly traditional, but he was trying to push people into different approaches to the traditional. Will Ransom, one of Goudy's early partners, put it more clearly than Goudy did. Noting, in his introduction to the catalogue of the American Institute of Graphic Arts' 1933 retrospective of the work of the Village Press, that Goudy's beginnings were in "the profession of lettering and design for advertising," Ransom wrote:

To the profession (or, preferably, art) he brought a fresh impulse to work radical changes in the methods of type design — no less than the idea that letters should be drawn, *produced in freedom by coordination of eye and hand and taste, rather than constructed by rule and line. That freedom is common practice nowadays, but it was an innovation then, a revolutionary injection of personal interpretation into established forms. Where earlier type designers usually followed the practice of translating written letters or previous type faces, he proposed the theorem of* intentional design *in letter construction — and proved it.*

Goudy's rejection of geometrical rules was a denial of the practice of most of his contemporaries.

Above: Goudy's demonstration of the development of the letter g from seventh-century uncials to the twentieth century, from The Alphabet

Right: Goudy at his matrix-engraving machine

omnia gubernare dicimus a quo iteriora mens mittitur ad omnia:quæ
ad cõmunicationem illius o dinata sût.Quom igitur ad nos cõuersus
deus respiciat nos tum ipsius radiis sit ut uiuamus:corpora quoq; alãt
ac uiuant.Quom uero in altitudinem suam deus se ipsum conuertat:
tunc corpora quidem extiguuntur:mens uero uiuit uita beatiore.Ista
illis psalmistæ similia sunt. Quã magnificata sunt opera tua domine:
omnia in sapientia fecisti:impleta eft terra possessione tua:omnia a te
expectant ut des illi escam in tempore:dante te illi colligent:aperiente
te manum tuam omnia implebuntur bonitate.Auertente auté te facié
turbabuntur:auferes spiritum eorum:& deficient:& in puluerem suû
reuertentur.Emitte spiritũ tuũ:& creabuntur:& renouabis facié terræ.
Quid eni hæc ab illis differũt:quom philosophus asserat respiciéte deo
uiuunt ipsius radiis animalia:cõuerso auté i suã altitudiné extinguũt?

He clearly had some mathematical rules in mind, but he refused rulers and compasses. And he would not copy directly from older typefaces. Earlier, Morris and his colleagues had used photographic enlargements of classic types and made drawings on them to create new faces, and Bruce Rogers did the same thing much later. If Goudy wanted to study an old type, he would draw versions of it freehand. His drawings of the Jenson face that survive are clearly his own handiwork, but they reveal some characteristics of Jenson, such as curve stresses and direction of the axis of letters, that are not more evident in photographic enlargements of the letters than they are on the page. Obviously, such slight accentuations of these characteristics as appear in the Goudy drawings also tell one something about Goudy's own imagination.

Goudy not only insisted that he was right to take such freedoms in designing types; he thought all designers should. At the time, the foundries had many people who were adroit in changing older faces in small ways so the foundries could justify selling them as new faces. If one accepted such small adjustments as invention, we would have to say that Morris Benton of American Type Founders created at least two hundred faces. (In fact he made some changes in a few famous old types that, to adapt Dr. Johnson's praise of an editor of Shakespeare, raise the corrector to the level of the inventor.) Goudy was not always gentle with such people; he said with annoyance that they would tinker with an edge or add a curlicue and call the result a new type. That was unacceptable. For Goudy, the designer — unlike a typographer, who might make minor adjustments in an existing type to achieve certain results in a single project — had to start every new face from the beginning. On the other hand, his claims for originality were limited; he told students at Washington and Lee University:

In the strictest sense of the

Below: Goudy's drawings of
Jenson
Opposite: A passage from
Eusebius, De evangelica prae-
paratione, *printed by Nicolaus*
Jenson, Venice, 1470

Itaქ ab Hom
eloquentia co

words probably no one ever re-
ally designs a type, since, after
all, what we call "an original
typeface" is undoubtedly little more
than a subtle variation of an ortho-
dox or traditional letter-form, a
form that we strive to endow with
a charm of character or a quality
of personality, and our efforts
sometimes achieve, unconsciously,
a measure of originality.[6]

How much originality was desirable, or what kind of originality, is another matter. Goudy wanted
originality kept firmly within one

great tradition. He would have
disputed that statement. But in
fact he had little patience with
some of the newer expressions.
He never designed — and probably never even had any feeling
for — a good sans serif. His bold
faces generally reveal an impatience with, if not a distaste for,
heavy faces. His black, or fraktur,
faces he generally considered sports.
So there was in general one good
tradition for him. And within that,
there were good and bad models.

He singled out Garamond,

Bodoni, Didot, Caslon, and Baskerville as makers of types a printer
could use for almost any purposes
satisfactorily. But then he added
that the clothes worn in Elizabe-
than times were also satisfactory.
Style, however, has its claim on
us: "Why carry loyalty to the point
of disregarding all newer designs,
when possibly some may be equally
meritorious?" To be sure, Goudy
had the gravest objections to the
last four of the five makers of
satisfactory types in his catalogue.
Baskerville he faulted for differ-

ences in the weights of capitals
and lower case that made his pages
spotty. Caslon he criticized often
for designing letters that could
not be composed into easily readable lines and for capitals that too
often did not fit well with his lower
case. Didot was derived from Bodoni, and, as for Bodoni, Goudy
thought in 1918 that "his types
are absolutely devoid of any artistic quality, being so regular and
precise in line that a monotonous
effect is produced." He objected
to the attenuation of the thin lines

in Bodoni's types, "with a reduction of the graduated portion of
the curves to a minimum," and
found a page of Bodoni "a maze
of heavy lines fretted here and
there with grayness, so that the
eye is constantly readjusting its
focus." He did allow that the effect of Bodoni's types on the page
was "brilliant." But when he revised
The Alphabet twenty years later,
he kept his original opinion of
Bodoni.

Five up, four down. So, what
was the right tradition, or how
did one connect with it? First, it
was a good idea to study the old
manuscript hands from which the
earliest type designers had drawn
their inspiration, if indeed they
had not simply copied some of
them. His own remarks on writing and the development of letters reveal a solid knowledge of
those hands. But he said that, for
himself, the handwriting was not
very inspirational, that he got a
good deal more out of studying
the typefaces of people like Jenson, Aldus, Garamond, and many
others. If he was looking to handmade letters for inspiration, it was
invariably to those of the Greeks
and Romans and mostly to inscriptional forms:

*Letters, to be classic, need not
be cast in Greek or Latin mold; if
they are expressed clearly, as a
Greek or Roman might have rendered them, with entire freedom
from whims and with a realization
of the necessity for directness, no
frigid adherence or pedantic prejudice for the Greek or Latin forms
themselves is essential. Classicism, therefore, is not the mere
reproduction of those creations,
but, instead, is the craftsman's
individual re-expression, in the
spirit of the classical, of the thought
underlying those ancient characters.*

Bodoni

When a type design is good, it is not because each individual letter
of the alphabet is perfect in form but because there is a feeling of unbroken
harmony and rhythm that runs through the whole design,
each letter to every other and to all.
ABCDEFGHIJKLMNOPQRSTUVWXYZ
abcdefghijklmnopqrstuvwxyz
0123456789

Caslon

When a type design is good, it is not because each individual letter
of the alphabet is perfect in form but because there is a feeling of unbroken
harmony and rhythm that runs through the whole design,
each letter to every other and to all.
ABCDEFGHIJKLMNOPQRSTUVWXYZ
abcdefghijklmnopqrstuvwxyz
0123456789

Baskerville

When a type design is good, it is not because each individual letter
of the alphabet is perfect in form but because there is a feeling of unbroken
harmony and rhythm that runs through the whole design,
each letter to every other and to all.
ABCDEFGHIJKLMNOPQRSTUVWXYZ
abcdefghijklmnopqrstuvwxyz
0123456789

Garamond

When a type design is good, it is not because each individual letter
of the alphabet is perfect in form but because there is a feeling of unbroken
harmony and rhythm that runs through the whole design,
each letter to every other and to all.
ABCDEFGHIJKLMNOPQRSTUVWXYZ
abcdefghijklmnopqrstuvwxyz
0123456789

Goudy annoyed even many of his friends when he insisted that no one could innovate from the classical models who was not a professional, and he defined a professional as someone who made his living from his craft. The self-justification in his definition offends, perhaps, but it does not invalidate his point. He was saying that a designer had to steep himself in the classical tradition until his innovations became natural — to him and to the tradition. He said of Jenson that he "had an instinctive sense of exact harmony in types, and he was so intent on legibility that he disregarded conformity to any standard — an innovation that modern designers might well consider."

Another way to put it is that he was trying to focus attention on the origins of the ornamental expression of language in writing and then in type and on the limitations inherent in that expression. As he got older he talked increasingly about type in terms of ordinary tools and household implements, and he emphasized that such things became traditional only through generations of use. In an oddly passionate statement of his case he said that tradition is "merely the ladder by which we climb, the working hypothesis that saves us from despair because it is all we have to go on." If anyone wonders why academic critics, or people who have never worked as printers or type designers, tend to dislike Goudy's attitude, that remark ought to let them know Goudy was aware of that reaction. He added that restraint should not dull the craft of the worker within a tradition: "A wholesome respect for the thought and effort that has brought about a tradition will go far to prevent the perpetration of eccentric solecisms." That

Bodoni

Caslon

Baskerville

Garamond

Above and opposite: Monotype settings of Bodoni, Caslon, Baskerville, and Garamond

is a nice point, a knife to the ribs.

On the other hand, the professional type designer was to command a good deal more than a knowledge of letters:

The immediate business of an artist may be the practice of but one craft, but unless his interest is concerned with the whole range of art, he will fall short of attaining the fullest ideals of his own. If he would express in his work vivacity, charm, invention, grace, and an interesting variety, he must cultivate a fine taste and a liberal spirit by a study of the masterpieces of all the arts. He will thus gain a breadth and depth of vision, an insight into fundamental principles, and the courage to face technical difficulties. He must learn, however, not to imitate masterpieces, but rather to follow the traditions on which masterpieces are reared. Tradition, we see then, is a matter of environment and of intellectual atmosphere. The continuous efforts of generations of cunning workers along one line led naturally to the accumulation of knowledge, increased ability to design, and greater manual dexterity, so that certain ways of doing things have come to be recognized as the best. Therefore, it is only by following good and tried traditions that craftsmanship of the highest order can come.

Goudy was being cautious, perhaps even reverent, in an age of the expansion of limitless expectations. "Once in a blue moon an individual designer will distinguish himself by his personal choice and unusual treatment of details," he said, "by some new thought or method, or by a fresh sentiment or point of view." It was not as an afterthought that he linked that caution with what he counted on his audience understanding: "Hap-

pily, the imaginative faculty is not confined to a few, since in some degree it belongs to all, a common heritage that grows with use. A sound tradition directs the imagination and confines it safely within the bounds of reason." That is an argument for tradition that has great power. Goudy was much older than most students are when they become steeped in a culture in the way he meant them to be, so some of what he said may have expressed his hope that others might have an earlier introduction to it. But he did have an advantage in coming to his studies late. One never meets wisdom young, and it is not certain that he thought earlier saturation would make a better craftsman.

However he got wisdom, the craftsman equipped with the proper culture and instincts might produce a good type. The standard was readability, and although Goudy was often imprecise in his definition of that word, it is not difficult to understand what he meant. His imprecision comes, again, from his predilection for the old classic typefaces. His remark that if letters are rendered "as a Greek or Roman" might have fashioned them makes the point. It is a point that separates Goudy today from the majority, who feel a terrific force operating against any recognition of a past achievement as a standard. But such matters of taste are more the result of purely intellectual fashion than of changes in life that dictate whole styles, and they change rather quickly; it is worthwhile to understand Goudy's standard, which he tried to base on something more substantial.

It is not beside the point to notice here that, for all his insistence on tradition and classicism, Goudy was not doctrinaire about the traditional methods of print-

ABDEGNRS

SQVE·ROMAN\
N·ERVAE·F·NERVAE
RM·DACICO·PONTIF
XVIII·IMP·VI·COS·VI·PP
VANTAE·ALTITVDINIS
IBVS·SIT·EGESTVS

Above: Inscription on Trajan's Column in Rome, second century A.D.
Opposite: Goudy's drawings of capitals from the column, from The Alphabet and Elements of Lettering. *The resulting type was called Trajan Title and issued in 1930*

After this he lifted up his head, and seeing the moon rising, walked towards the palace. As he passed through the fields, and saw the animals around him, "Ye, said he, are happy, and need not envy me that walk thus among you, burthened with myself; nor do I, ye gentle ones, envy your felicity; for it is not the felicity of man. I have many distresses from which ye are free; I fear pain when I do not feel it: I sometimes shrink at evils recollected, and sometimes start at evils anticipated: surely the equity of providence has balanced peculiar sufferings with peculiar joys

Above: A passage from Philip Rusher's Rasselas *of 1804, set in a typeface designed by Rusher that was intended to be totally original. Goudy called it "more interesting than beautiful"*

ing, as many of his contemporaries were. In a hand-printed book there is the experience of a tactile sense of reading, and that is important to an understanding of Goudy's ideas about type. He printed many of his own books by hand and had a passion for the old books. He insisted, when he cut his own matrices, that he could feel the difference between one thousandth of an inch and two thousandths in the edge of the typeface. But all his life he was trying to discover and formulate rules for people whose printing might be done in many ways other than the traditional ones. His principle of legibility is important to understand, at some length, in his own words:

Pleasing legibility is the fore- *most consideration. One offense to avoid is extreme attenuation of any lines, as this involves constant alteration of the focus of the eyes, which, though slight in the reading of a few words or a line, is extremely wearing in the aggregate....*

In the first place, simplicity of form is necessary; this requires a study of the essential root forms, which are practically those of the lapidary capitals of two thousand years ago. Each of those characters had an individuality. By emphasizing this characteristic quality in such a way that nothing in it inclines us to confound any letter with its neighbor, we may get a new impression or quality of personality, which is as far as we may go, since *those forms are now fixed.... Beauty, too, is desirable, but beauty must not be emphasized if it detracts from easy readability. Beauty is an inherent characteristic of simplicity, dignity, harmony, proportion, strength — qualities always found in an easily legible type; yet legibility is seldom achieved by a predetermined effort to produce it. To attempt consciously to give a specific character or beauty to a letter is too frequently, also, to exhibit the intellectual process by which it is sought; its character seems to have been thought in & does not appear to be the outcome of a subtle and indefinable taste that makes it delightful & seemingly the obvious and inevitable thing.*

When he turned to defining legibility in later years Goudy often cited very old formulations. That was deliberate. He knew many of the current studies on the subject, psychological and otherwise. When he opened a chapter in *Typologia* with a citation from a French cleric about what made the eye tired in reading, he was being funny and serious at the same time. The passage he quoted from Ancillon was famous, but Goudy was using it to declare which camp he stood in: "The less the eye is fatigued in reading a book, the more at liberty the mind is to judge of it."

He frequently warned type designers not to become enchanted with letters; if they were to be of use to readers they could only design whole alphabets because it

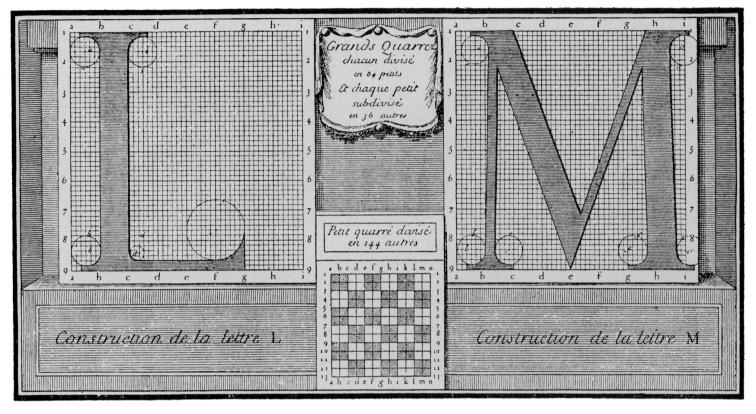

*Above: In 1694 the French sci-
entist Jaugeon recommended
"the projection of every Roman
capital on a framework of 2,304
little squares"*

might be possible to design twenty-
six very beautiful letters that would
baffle and tire the eye of the reader.
His constant insistence that the
mind perceives words, not letters,
seems a bit schoolmasterish until
one looks at many modern books
and magazines and newspapers.
The number of typefaces that are
bothersome to read seems to be
increasing exponentially, and one
can only conclude that many designers ignore what Goudy defined
as their first duty, "to combat any
attempt to interfere materially with
the accepted medium of intellectual exchange." The notion that
type designer, typographer, compositor, and printer were all guardi-
ans of literature and thought is
essential in Goudy's dicta about
design. He could also be ferociously

*Above: Herbert Bayer's 1925
Universal lower-case-only typeface in bold wide and condensed bold, a modern attempt to
create a rational typeface*

impatient with anyone who thought
the work of such professionals could
be, or should be, trivial.

As for the letters themselves:

*Legibility depends on three
things: first, simplicity, that is, a
form having no unnecessary parts;
second, contrast, as shown by
marked differences in the weight
of the lines composing the individual letters (stems and hairlines), and also as shown in the
varying widths of different letters; and third, proportion, each
part of a letter having its proper
value and relation to the other
parts and to other letters — these
three things in connection with
the aspects of purpose and use.*

He encouraged type designers
to seek beauty, but only with great
care; every change made in the

essential form of a letter in pur-
suit of beauty endangers legibility. On a practical level, he also
advised typemakers to avoid extreme polish, arguing that some
of the accidental qualities of their
work would be lost if they refined
every curve and stroke too much;
they might sacrifice the individual character of their work, which
is really the expression of their
art. He has a striking formula-
tion — unsettling, but quite profound — that has serious impli-
cations in an age when technology is becoming increasingly an
extension of one's fingertips, if
not of one's brain, erasing the re-
sistance of matter in the creation
of that most plastic creature, type:
"The limitations of equipment and
materials made the productions

of the first printers beautiful because the resulting restraint and harmony compelled style."

Yet Goudy was acutely aware that no definition of readability, let alone of beauty, is exclusive. In *Typologia* he wrote a fine and amusing survey of designers and theorists who for four hundred years tried to arrive at a scientific definition of readability, only to have their speculations made ridiculous by designers who followed their rules. He is entertaining about the schemes of the French scientist Jaugeon in the seventeenth century, which involved creating roman capitals on a framework of 2,304 little squares and the lower case and italic letters on systems of geometric shapes so complex that they could scarcely be comprehended, and about the attempt of Philip Rusher in England in the nineteenth century to create a type never seen before. But his most telling pages contain his analysis of the failures of William Morris, C. W. Ricketts, C. R. Ashbee, and others — people who in fact had first stimulated his own interest in type. His melancholy conclusion was that, since the creation of Caslon's old style type in 1724, "we have gradually drifted away from the canons of easy legibility."

His only suggestion for improving readability was to try better types. It is hard to think of any other way, and perhaps his candor ought to be appreciated. If readers of papers and magazines, who think them quite readable, were to have them replaced with similar publications in a superior type, he said, after a time they would realize how unreadable was the type they had become accustomed to. He said with some acerbity that "the customs of the igno-

rant" were not proper standards. His own standard was:

...a type without mannerisms, one that is easily and pleasantly readable, masculine, its forms distinct and not made to display the skill of the designer, but instead to help the reader. Type must be easy to read, graceful, but not weak; decorative, but not ornate; beautiful in itself and in composition; austere and formal, with no stale or uninteresting regularity in its irregular parts; simple in design, but not with the bastard simplicity of form which is mere crudity of outline; elegant, that is, gracious in line and fluid in form; and above all it must possess unmistakably the quality we call "art" — that something which comes from the spirit the designer puts unconsciously into the body of his work.

Goudy's rules for good printing and typography are very much of a piece with that. He scorned designers of books or printers who forgot that their purpose was to express not their ideas but those of the author of the book. His contempt arose from his feeling that it is so much easier for a typographer or printer to draw attention to his own work than to the ideas of the writer, and he was always suspicious of easy ways. What he wanted was style:

The living expression controlling both the form and the vital structure of the means by which the idea is presented — a quality inseparable from the work of a craftsman wholly unconscious of style or of any definite aim toward beauty. It is that subtle attribute of printing which relates it to the time of the actual worker in the craft, as influenced by his environment and the stress of necessity.

Goudy was naturally good humored but also exasperatingly independent, and what he was really claiming for type designers and typographers was that they were artists. He had so much authority for a couple of decades that if he had laid down clear rules for design they would have been taken very seriously. He knew his own practices well and could describe them fully. But, to a great age, he continued to demolish what were taken as the most important pronouncements on the design of type, even as he chided designers and printers alike for their insensitivity to tradition, standards, beauty, and the very materials they were working with. His good humor makes his prodding especially sharp. One can read through dozens of his talks and all his pamphlets and books and ask again and again: All right, what should be done? Goudy never answers, but asks another question or questions another long-accepted rule. In that sense he was a good old-fashioned teacher.

In the end one is struck by his restraint. Withholding judgment gave little comfort to his friends or to him. The ordinary way of building up people's reputations in his age, as now, was for the most conspicuous people in any coterie to praise the work of others constantly and for the others to respond with more praise of the praiser. The method is obvious. Goudy did little of that. He was quite generous to everyone, but when he began to talk about specific types he usually confined himself to discussions of the classic faces or his own designs. Since his death it has been easy for people to translate that habit into mere egotism and self-promotion. Goudy had enough of both. But it is clear

The King's fount by Sir Charles Ricketts, of which Goudy observed in Typologia, *"His intention was in the right direction, but it seems to me that it was carried out ineptly"*

Vale type by Sir Charles Ricketts, an earlier face from which the King's fount evolved

Motteroz type, 1876, chosen by the Municipal Council of Paris for official publications for its readability, "a conclusion that is not shared by me, since I do not find [it] essentially legible" Goudy wrote in Typologia

Golden type by William Morris. Goudy found that, "His handling of certain details in some letters actually gives them an appearance of clumsiness." He conceded that, "It was legible and it was an innovation"

Endeavour type by C. R. Ashbee, a disciple of Morris. Goudy said, "[Ashbee] seems to have had the idea that type is beautiful only as it defies easy reading"

from any fair reading of what he had to say about design that his passion was to get some real argument started about the history of design, its standards, the rationale of it, and whether it could be approached philosophically or theoretically at all.

The apostolic Goudy was a very good influence and one that ought to be revived. There are no answers, I think, to the questions he often raised about esthetics. But there are important questions left

"Awak! awake! I bring, lufar, I bring
The newis glad, that blisfull ben and sure
Of thy confort: now lauch, and play, and syng,
That art besid so glad an auenture;

Haec honorum caelestium ad puellae mortalis culti
modica translatio uerae Veneris uehementer incendit anii
inpatiens indignationis capite quassanti fremens altius sic
disserit, 'en rerum naturae prisca parens, en elementorum

CLAUDE MOTTEROZ was born in
1830, at Romanèche (Saône-et-Loire).
As the descendant of an old family of
printers he was taught printing, to

THE CRONYCLES OF SYR JOHN
FROISSART, translated by John Bourchier,
Lord Berners. Reprinted from Pynson's Edi-
tion of 1523 and 1525. Edited by Halliday Spar-

Of the vellum series the following will probably appear in the course of the next two years, and
with the work, it is hoped, of the artists whose
names are appended, they having promised

and, what is more significant, new questions to be raised all the time that no one is now thinking about.

It is in many ways more satisfying, and certainly more comforting, to read William Morris, Stanley Morison, Daniel Berkeley Updike, C. R. Ashbee — almost anyone from Goudy's era — than it is to read Goudy on the principles of type. Almost any of his contemporaries had much more articulate notions about what was right. But Goudy always asked better questions. Morris and Ashbee both designed types that can now be seen as, at best, quaint. Updike wrote a wonderful history of type and printing, and he sponsored types for his Merrymount Press that are simply unusable. Morison, finally engaged in the design of a type for a newspaper, produced with his team Times Roman, which is perhaps more familiar to readers around the world today than any other face but which is a book face, not a newspaper face, and which has made many a publication look archly important but oddly unearthly. Goudy was the only one among the leading figures of his time who would tempt the wrath of powerful people by pointing out that a face that is good for a book is probably terrible for advertising or newspapers or magazines and that there is a standard for every means of expression, as there are different environments for different publications.

It is his fate to have annoyed the people he was closest to, the everyday workingmen, by refusing to give them rules from on high and to have enraged his peers in the design business by insisting that design is in fact a business but designers have to be artists. Goudy is never comforting, but he is the one person of that era in that game to whom you have to go back constantly to be sure you know all the questions you should be asking yourself.

Left and above: Goudy over the years

By his own account Goudy was forty-six years old when he stopped being an amateur and took up type designing as a profession.[7] Indeed, he was thirty when he first drew an alphabet that a foundry bought and cast into type. If there is anything in his youth that explains the extraordinary career he took up in middle age, it seemed to have escaped his memory — and everyone else's. In 1939 his friend Vrest Orton talked to people who had known Goudy as a student at the Shelbyville, Illinois, high school. Orton reported that "not a single schoolmate of his in those days saw a great future" for Goudy. One woman remembered him as strange. "We all liked him," she said, "but somehow he was always a little queer." The artist Robert Root, another classmate, said that "Goudy was no unusual lad. I would have said he was destined to become a sign painter."[8]

Goudy was no more informative. He remembered winning a first prize in a county drawing contest and recalled that when he was ten he could make "creditable pencil copies of wood-engravings found in the magazines of the '70s, and, strangely enough,

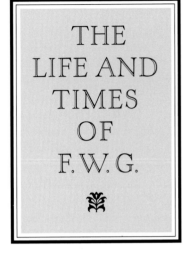

THE LIFE AND TIMES OF F.W.G.

after copying one of these carefully, I could make a good facsimile of it from memory. But as I remember, any *creative* instinct at this time seemed absolutely lacking in my make-up." One talent he had from an early age that was to serve him well in making types was a strong instinct for mechanical things; he even intended for a time to become a mechanical engineer.

Goudy was born in Bloomington, Illinois, on March 8, 1865, as the Civil War was drawing to a close. Christened Frederic William, he was one of three children, two boys and a girl, of John Fleming Goudy and Amanda Melvina Truesdell Goudy. In 1865, his father still spelled the name Gowdy; he changed it only in about 1883 (there are many variants of this name both in Scotland and in the United States). John Goudy had come to Illinois from Ohio where his father, Thomas Biggar Goudy, was a farmer. Thomas may have been an immigrant from Scotland, but in his accounts of his own background Goudy simply said his grandfather was "of Scottish descent." At the time of Goudy's birth, John Goudy was the superintendent of schools in Bloomington. He moved his family to several other downstate Illinois cities before he went to Highmore, in what was still the Dakota Territory, in 1884. In Dakota he established a real estate business and was for a time a probate judge, but later in his life he returned to school administration.

It was only in Shelbyville that Goudy located some roots of his later fascination with letters and drawing. His favorite story about his youth concerned his decoration of a Presbyterian Sunday School room when he was sixteen years old. He had proposed to fill in spaces between the windows with the Ten Commandments cut out of colored paper and glued to the walls. The project grew until he had to cut three-thousand characters for the Biblical verses he put up. His work had disappeared under a heavy coat of paint by the 1930s when a disciple went to Shelbyville with an offer to pay for restoration of the room as a shrine only to discover that the paint could not be removed without destroying the letters under it. The only other lettering he recalled making as a boy was done just before he moved to Dakota. "Our local baker had got a new delivery wagon and asked me if I could paint his name on each side of it. I did, using what today would be called sans-serif letter — then it was known as 'block letter.'" Presumably Root had that wagon in mind when he told Orton he thought Goudy would become a sign painter.

In Highmore, Goudy worked for four years in his father's real estate office, principally as a bookkeeper. But he also began doing the layouts for the many different forms the business needed and later said that "unconsciously, I

was developing a flair for typographic arrangement." Typography was not in his mind as a way of making a living, however; in 1888 he tried to establish a loan and mortgage company and, when the plan did not work out, he moved to Minneapolis and became a department store bookkeeper. The next year he moved on to Springfield, Illinois, to work in a real estate office, and in a few months he left for Chicago.

Anyone with even a latent interest in design could hardly have avoided being excited by Chicago in 1890. The city was swept up in planning the Columbian Exposition of 1893, and design, of everything from buildings to clothes, was the topic of the day. In the event, that world's fair had a very long-lasting effect on the appearance of this country. Some of that effect was execrable, but the newspaper and magazine battles about design between the florid neoclassicists and the leaders of the new school of Chicago architecture remain memorable, especially the contributions of some of the losers, people who nevertheless became powerful voices for new design in the next century.

The movement that John Ruskin and William Morris had championed in England took root in this country first in Chicago. In the 1890s craft and design shops were everywhere in the city, from Jane Addams's Hull House to Clara Barck Welles's great Kalo silver shops, which continued producing handwrought silver remarkable for its original designs until 1970 (Mrs. Welles, three years Goudy's junior, lived to be ninety-seven, and the shops outlived her only five years). Even the large department stores had their own handcraft shops where original design was highly prized.

It was assumed in that age that design was a unity and that people could pass from one part of it to another without much inconvenience. In 1890, for instance, Frank Lloyd Wright was eminent as a designer in metal, ceramics, and glass; later, as an architect, he used his talents in those materials to spectacular effect. His mentor, the architect Louis Sullivan, was no mean decorative designer himself. It was Sullivan and a few other architects who set the agenda for the discussion of all design in

Top: The Columbian Exposition of 1893, Chicago
Opposite, top: Louis Sullivan's Auditorium Theater, Chicago
Above: William Morris flanked by his wife May Morris and the printer Sir Emery Walker, September 1895
Opposite, bottom: The opening chapter of William Morris's The Story of the Glittering Plain, *1890, the first book published by Morris at the Kelmscott Press*

A Table of the Chapters of this Book.

I. Of those Three who came to the House of the Raven, 1. ❡ II. Evil Tidings come to hand at Cleveland, 4. ❡ III. The Warriors of the Raven search the Seas, 9. ❡ IV. Hallblithe taketh the Sea, 12. ❡ V. They come unto the Isle of Ransom, 15. ❡ VI. Of a Dwelling of Men on the Isle of Ransom, 28. ❡ VII. A Feast in the Isle of Ransom, 37. ❡ VIII. Hallblithe taketh Ship again from the Isle of Ransom, 51. ❡ IX. They come to the Land of the Glittering Plain, 56. ❡ X. They hold Converse with Folk of the Glittering Plain, 66. ❡ XI. The Sea-eagle reneweth his Life, 73. ❡ XII. They look on the King of the Glittering Plain, 79. ❡ XIII. Hallblithe beholdeth the woman who loveth him, 86. ❡ XIV. Hallblithe has speech with the King again, 93. ❡ XV. Yet Hallblithe speaketh with the King, 101. ❡ XVI. Those Three go their ways to the edge of the Glittering Plain, 106. ❡ XVII. Hallblithe amongst the Mountains, 113. ❡ XVIII. Hallblithe dwelleth in the wood alone, 126. ❡ XIX. Hallblithe builds him a skiff, 134. ❡ XX. So now saileth Hallblithe away from the Glittering Plain, 143. ❡ XXI. Of the Fight of the Champions in the Hall of the Ravagers, 157. ❡ XXII. They go from the Isle of Ransom and come to Cleveland by the Sea, 178.

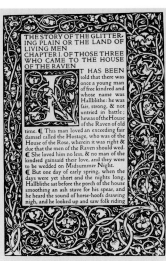

those days; they had deep influence on the thriving school of lettering in Chicago, a school rightly, and for reasons beyond what the designation usually implies, known as a school of architectural lettering. Today one has only to look up at the letters of the somewhat mystical sayings Sullivan applied to the great gold-leafed walls of his Auditorium Theater to see his vision of the integrity of graphic design and architecture.

Of more immediate importance to Goudy's future, Chicago was then the largest printing center in the United States. His first job there had little to do with printing directly. He became private secretary to Richard Coe Alden, a financial broker, whom he had met when Alden acted as the agent for the sale of Dakota farm mortgages negotiated by Goudy and his father. "Since he was familiar with some of the layouts I had made," Goudy said, "he had me arrange and have printed for him the prospectuses of his clients, and in this way I came into contact with several Chicago printers." In Alden's office he came into contact, as well, with a secretary, Bertha Matilda Sprinks. It took him seven years to make up his mind but he finally married Bertha.

After less than a year with Alden, Goudy was back in real estate, where he stayed four years. But his interest immediately became concentrated on his advertisements. He gained a reputation for ingenuity and clarity in typography among the printers, and editorials in their magazine, *The Inland Printer*, began to praise his work. That spur of admiration moved him to start a magazine in 1892, *Modern Advertising*. It lasted only a few issues, but it brought him the acquaintance of the advertising managers of the city's largest manufacturing and merchandising companies, who were to be his patrons for some years. More important, through it he met Will Bradley, whose ingenious design work Goudy was to praise and imitate for years. It was Bradley who first had the notion of designing an entirely new cover for each issue of a magazine, and *The Inland Printer* was the publication he chose for his series of impressive experiments. Goudy often acknowledged personal inspiration from Bradley, but the model of Bradley's work was even more important.

For a few months during one of his early years in Chicago Goudy also had a job in a secondhand bookstore, where, he always said, he learned a great deal about books. He learned more at the one operated by the A. C. McClurg publishing house, where he became part of the coterie around George Millard, who operated a section of the store he called the Saints and Sinners Corner. Millard educated his customers about book

design and types and was an apostle for the ideas of Morris. It was Millard who introduced Goudy to books from the Kelmscott Press and other private presses in England, and he and a number of Chicago writers in the group also led Goudy to the Newberry Library, where he first began studying Renaissance books.

One book Goudy encountered in the Saints and Sinners Corner was *The Songs and Poems of Sir John Suckling*, printed in the Vale type designed by Charles Ricketts and Charles James Cobden-Sanderson, with woodcut borders and initials by Ricketts. Goudy, who said he first saw it "about 1895" (in fact it was published in 1896), considered it "typographic glory" at the time. His copy of it has an inscription to Edmund Geiger Gress, then editor of *The American Printer*, dated November 3, 1923: "This is the book that over 20 years ago inspired in me an interest in typography for itself — an interest which has increased with years, and, I hope, has lead to a great knowledge & taste of bookish things on my part."[9] Ricketts is the man who, shortly before he died, dumped all his types into the Thames to keep them out of the hands of the philistines. People who know Goudy's later work, in printing as well as in design, may be a little surprised to find that the Suckling volume inspired him; it is a very dark and, by later standards, undistinguished affair, but next to most of the commercially produced books of the time, it still looks quite striking.

Never in his life did Goudy say a word against the real estate game, but his own tastes were bound to take him out of it. Late in 1894 he persuaded C. Lauron Hooper, a schoolteacher he had met several

years before, to back him financially, and the two set up the Booklet Press in an office on South Dearborn Street, where the printing trades were concentrated. Goudy immediately expanded his reputation among the printers. For his press's first booklet he chose a nine-point type but found that the letters took up more room than he wanted them to, so he measured the type and then ordered it cast on an eight-point body. His concern with getting a close fitting of letters would last all his life and lead to a few notable failures and some important successes.

That same year Herbert S. Stone

and Ingalls Kimball, students at Harvard College, founded a literary magazine, *The Chap-Book*. Its first appearance attracted no notice in Boston, so they moved it to Chicago, where Stone also set up a publishing house. Goudy, ignoring the fact that he had not the equipment to make anything more than a pamphlet, bid for and won the contract to compose the magazine. During the year he produced it (once it grew in size and importance the magazine migrated for its printing to the firm of R. R. Donnelley & Sons), he learned a great deal about design and expanded his shop. He got another bonus from the experience as well.

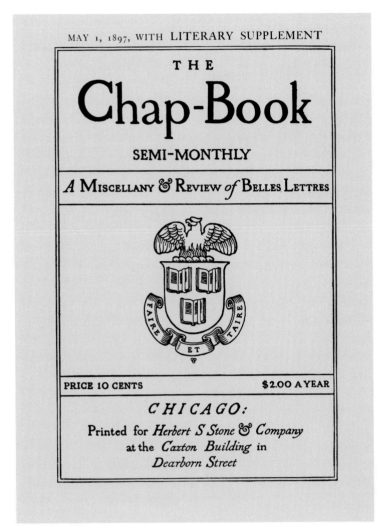

MAY 1, 1897, WITH LITERARY SUPPLEMENT

THE
Chap-Book

SEMI-MONTHLY

A MISCELLANY *&* REVIEW *of* BELLES LETTRES

FAIRE ET TAIRE

PRICE 10 CENTS $2.00 A YEAR

CHICAGO:
Printed for *Herbert S Stone & Company*
at the *Caxton Building* in
Dearborn Street

Goudy and Hooper changed the name of their press to Camelot when they moved into a building named for the fifteenth-century printer William Caxton, and the name of the press became attached to the first type cut from Goudy's drawings. In 1896 Goudy drew an alphabet of capitals in a couple of hours and sent them to the Dickinson Foundry in Boston with a note asking whether they were worth five dollars. Dickinson sent him ten dollars, and his capitals shortly afterward appeared in the American Type Founders specimen book as Camelot. He immediately drew two more alphabets and sent them along to Dickinson, but nothing came of them. The face he later called Display Roman dates from that same period, as does his De Vinne Roman, a book face commissioned by Walter Marder of the Central Type Foundry in St. Louis who wanted a book face based on a widely used display type made by Theodore De Vinne.

Throughout his career Goudy was to design type ornaments, and for some years he was sought as a decorator of book and magazine covers. This is a skill he acquired in 1896, and, because there has been confusion about the matter in articles about Goudy during his life and since his death, it is worthwhile setting down his account:

While operating the Camelot Press I found it hard at times to get little bits of decorative material I thought might add to the appearance of the work in hand. Typefounders' ornaments in the years of the fin de siècle were as a rule stiff, often crude, and too trite for my taste. I had in my employ a young man named Berne Nadal, of French descent.... He did have some facility of design,

and occasionally would supply a bit of decoration that I would use.... And really it is due to him that I, later, became a decorative designer.

The brochure the Camelot Press issued at its start announced that "we hope to inculcate in those for whom printing is done a love of harmony and simplicity." Apparently Chicago was not ready for reform, however; late in 1896 the press failed, and Goudy turned to free-lance designing to make a living until he accepted a job in the summer of 1897 as bookkeeper and cashier of *The Michigan Farmer.*

That may have been a job he felt obliged to take since, after many years of Bertha's company, he decided to marry her. From the time he met her in Alden's office he began to consider her, as he often said for more than forty years, his best friend. The recollections of the two of them by people who knew them later tend to confirm that statement. For the early 1890s, it was an unusual relationship. They seem to have spent a great deal of time together, quite a lot of it on bicycles they rode all over the city. A pattern of affectionate independence was established in their friendship that was to last four decades. They were married in June 1897 in the home of Bertha's mother in the Chicago suburb of Berwyn, just before they moved to Detroit, where *The Michigan Farmer* was published.

Goudy may have been hired to keep the books in order, but he later admitted that he quickly began to spend what he called "idle time" in the printing shop of the magazine, where he made "occasional" advertising layouts. One of the magazine's regular advertisers, Alfred Zenner, after watching him work on a layout, asked Goudy to

---

The Chap-Book was probably the most important avant garde literary publication in the country until it merged with *The Dial* in 1898. Its writers included H. G. Wells, Anatole France, Paul Verlaine, and Stephen Crane, and its illustrators T. P. Hapgood, Ricketts, Henri de Toulouse-Lautrec, Will Bradley, and Aubrey Beardsley. The influence of these artists, especially Beardsley, can be seen in Goudy's designs and illustrations for many years, and his proximity to such writers put him in good stead with many American writers, who were happy to have their work printed by his private press for some decades afterward.

Top: The Chap-Book, *May 1, 1897*
Above: Advertisement for the Camelot Press
Opposite: Modern Advertising, *November 1892*
Overleaf, left: The Inland Printer, *February 1898*
Overleaf, right: The Inland Printer, *June 1890*

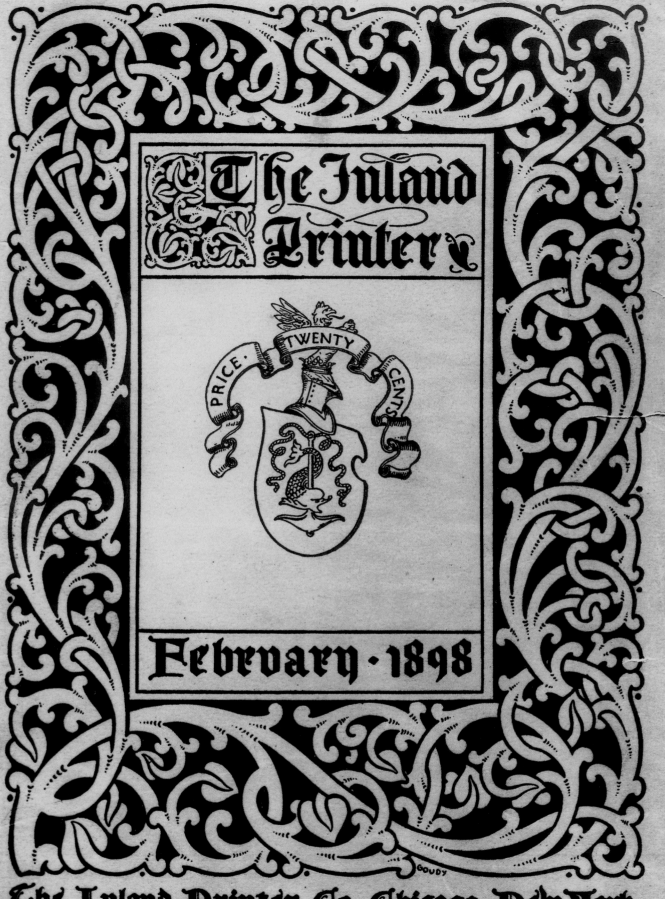

The Inland Printer

PRICE. TWENTY CENTS

February · 1898

GOUDY

The Inland Printer Co · Chicago · New York

The
INLAND
PRINTER
for June
MDCCCCC

A Technical Journal
devoted to PRINTING and the
ALLIED ARTS and published
Monthly by the Inland Printer
Company · Chicago & New York

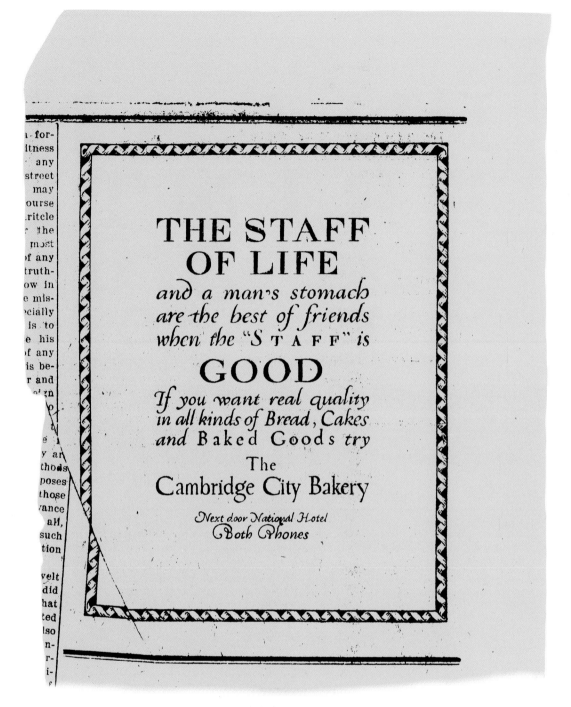

Above: "My first initial drawing 1893 or 4 FWG"
Right: Advertisement for the Cambridge City Bakery designed by Goudy
Opposite, left: Booklet for the Curtis Publishing Company, designed by Goudy
Opposite, right: Advertisement for the Zenner Disinfectant Company, designed by Goudy

design some materials for him as a free-lance job. One of his commissions, Goudy recalled almost fifty years later, led to criticism that "probably influenced me more in my lettering than any other single thing." Zenner looked at Goudy's design for a pamphlet cover and said, "You are not very strong on lower case, are you?" According to Goudy, that question "put me on my mettle and I began then seriously to study roman letter forms."

In 1898 Goudy lost his job at the magazine and, after working as a bookkeeper in Detroit for a few months, returned to Chicago to set up as a free lance. He must have been under some pressure since Bertha gave birth shortly after their return to their son, Frederic T. He seems to have had a great deal of work in the next eighteen months. Principally he made advertising lettering for such

companies as Hart Schaffner & Marx and the Kuppenheimer Company, clothing makers; the Marshall Field and Mandel Brothers department stores; and Lyon and Healy, a music publishing house. Advertisers, weary of the typographical messes that most pages were in those days, were eager to have their products appear in the clear, strong, distinctive pages Goudy could make for them.

He also worked on book covers. Before he left Detroit he had written to Thomas B. Mosher, the publisher and printer in Portland, Maine, asking for assignments. In 1899 he designed four covers for four little volumes in what Mosher called the Vest Pocket series. Mosher then asked him to design covers in a larger-format series, the Old World books, and it was through this commission that Goudy first became acquainted

SUCCESSFUL
DEALERS BELIEVE IN
WINDOW DISPLAY
ADVERTISING

THE CURTIS PUBLISHING COMPANY
PHILADELPHIA, PENNSYLVANIA

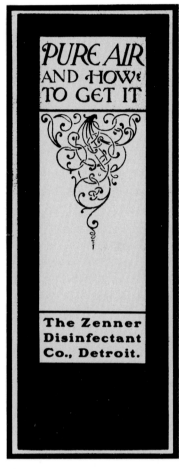

with the work of Bruce Rogers. Mosher wanted the lettering on the covers to harmonize with Rogers's letters on the title pages. Goudy said that was impossible: "Rogers already had developed a style that was his own and I could merely approximate it in appearance."

He was soon to discover that type foundries had no such nice standards as mere approximation. In 1900 Frank Holme, a newspaper artist who had founded the School of Illustration in Chicago, asked Goudy to become an instructor. There Goudy met W. W. Denslow, another newspaper artist, who had convinced McClure, Phillips and Company, a New York publisher, to issue an illustrated Mother Goose. Denslow asked Goudy to letter the book, and Goudy submitted a sample page that, he said, was appreciated for its appearance and for his speed of execution (he needed the money). For the project he developed a letter that was easy to do quickly, with short ascenders and descenders and a height in the short letters — the vowels, among others — that was noticeably high. "To my surprise," Goudy said, "a little later on, the Inland Type Foundry of St. Louis, without consultation with me, brought out a new type copied — not inspired — from my Denslow lettering, and added insult to injury by naming it Hearst."

There is some disagreement about what happened next between Goudy's account, written when he was eighty, and one written seventeen years earlier by his friend Peter Bielenson of the Peter Pauper Press. Goudy said that after this episode "type apparently occupied me not at all," although he allowed that his Pabst type may have been drawn at the time. The advertising manager of the Pabst

Below: American Cat News,
November 1900
Opposite: Printer's mark of the
Village Press, 1912

brewery had bought lettering from him through the J. Walter Thompson agency and later a department store executive asked whether it might be cast. Goudy made drawings of the letters and the store had American Type Founders cut several sizes of type. A.T.F. then asked Goudy to design a companion italic face and paid him one hundred dollars for it. (That was, Goudy said, "an unheard of figure… in those days.")

Bielenson's story is that, to compete with the Hearst type Inland issued, Goudy designed another. He began with the Mother Goose letters but gave them long ascenders and descenders. Once he had done that, his whole conception changed and he drew an entirely new alphabet, eventually producing the Pabst type. Bielenson's version is more convincing than Goudy's later one. First, he had to have had it from Goudy when he wrote it in 1938; a few of Goudy's old Chicago friends were still around then, but there is no indication anywhere in Bielenson's booklet that he had talked to any of them. Then, Goudy was always competitive, and at the time of the Mother Goose incident he was beginning to formulate a campaign to teach people that typefaces ought to be thought of, and created, as original designs. It was very common then for foundries to purloin one another's faces without giving credit or to tinker with details of an existing face and call it a new type. Goudy's growing impatience with the practice, combined with his outrage at Inland for taking over his drawings, makes Bielenson's story sound right.

Goudy's observation that Denslow appreciated his speed in lettering was ingenuous. He was notoriously dilatory about work. Lewis Hogarth Lozier, who shared a studio

Price, 10 Cents

American Cat News
CHICAGO, NOVEMBER, 1900

Published Monthly at 604 Cable Building, Chicago

with him, said Goudy once agreed to letter an elaborate wedding anniversary album for a railroad president for a hundred forty dollars — a fee so large that, when Lozier accepted it, Goudy began to wonder whether he should not charge more for all his work. He found every excuse to delay until he had less than a day to complete the job, and then he finished it in one burst.

Lozier, who had been a student at the School of Illustration in 1901 but not one of Goudy's pupils, mentioned to Holme that he was looking for a studio so he could go into business. Holme

introduced him to Goudy, who had the same idea, and they rented an office together. Lozier said:

We were together a year and a half… until the fall of 1902. We might have stayed together longer had he not acquired a severe attack of Angora Felinis…. He joined a cat club and took an active part in cat shows and cat club meetings, all to the detriment of his business. He was persuaded to start a cat magazine — The American Cat Journal — which didn't last as many months as a cat has lives. How he ever managed to bring out the three or four issues of the Journal *I could never make*

out. This magazine was issued before the Goudys started the Village Press, otherwise they would have published it and absorbed all the cost.

…I was working against time one warm afternoon when several cat people came into the office to talk over affairs of the Cat Club. Their chatter, in which Goudy was taking no part, got on my nerves and I could not concentrate on my work. Finally, I went out into the hall to get away from the distracting conversation. Fred sensed that I was disturbed and came out to apologize for his friends. Had I taken the matter as a joke, I think it would have prevented the break in our office relations. But I felt it was a detriment to his business to have that sort of thing going on in his office. I told him it should be stopped…. He said he didn't know of any way to stop it and would get out. There were no further words over the matter and Fred moved his effects to another location.[10]

There is a lot of Goudy in that story. There were many cats in his life. And he seldom got angry; he just moved on.

That move took him into book publishing. He had hovered around book publishing when he worked on cover designs for Stone — his cover for George Ade's *Fables in Spring* (1900) was something of a local sensation and Goudy always treasured it. In 1901 Kuppenheimer asked him to design a type for the company's advertising. Goudy drew letters based on Nicolas Jenson's fifteenth-century Venetian type — as modified, he was later to say, by Morris's Golden type, the Doves type, and many others, including Rogers's Montaigne. It probably owes most to the Morris Golden. In any case, what he drew was a book face, not a display, and Kuppenheimer turned it down.

A year later one of Goudy's students in the School of Illustration was Will Ransom, a young man from Snohomish, Washington, who had more money than Goudy had. When Goudy showed Ransom his drawings for Kuppenheimer, Ransom offered to have matrices cut and typecast. Thus Ransom became a partner briefly in the Village Press — the name came from the poem "The Village Blacksmith" — which Goudy was establishing with headquarters in the barn behind his house in Park Ridge, a Chicago suburb. The Village type was Goudy's mainstay for half a dozen years. It finally ended up in the possession of Frederick Fairchild Sherman, and unless his heirs allowed the matrices to be destroyed, that type still exists.

The Village Press began with an announcement of noble esthetic principles — and just as chaotically as all of Goudy's ventures would in the future. Shortly after its first book was issued — *Printing* by William Morris and Emery Walker — Goudy paid Ransom for the type and thus bought him out of the business, but Ransom was around long enough to collect some hilarious stories about the enthusiastic mayhem. The one aspect of its operation that was not chaotic was the composition. Bertha learned from the outset to set type and to fold, sew, and case in books by hand, and for thirty-two years she was the driving force behind the Village Press.

She would often bet Goudy she could perform intricate technical jobs as well as anyone, learning them on her own. She won her first bet with him the year before the press opened when she bought a Swedish loom and taught her-

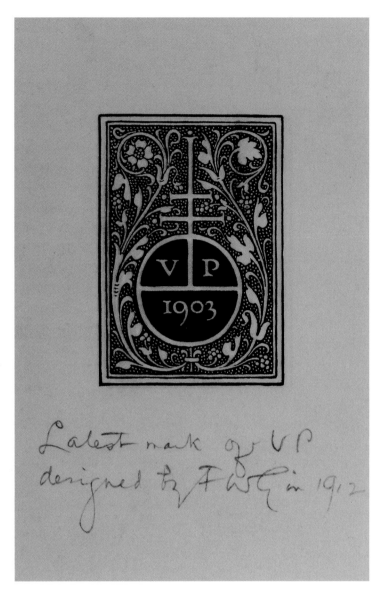

self to make rugs. Soon she taught him to make them too, and they made rugs for their home, and for sale — to help support their press. The Goudy who in later years was to become the apostle for the personal touch in all design was, at thirty-eight, a true-blue Morrisite. It is odd to think of Goudy weaving rugs, but he believed in crafts deeply, and long after Bertha died he recalled with pleasure that the loom was still packed away in his attic.

It was Bertha who then brought about a decisive change in their lives. She had read in a magazine about a burgeoning arts and crafts

colony in Hingham, Massachusetts. Goudy went there for an inspection, rented a house, and the family moved to Hingham in 1904. Neither Goudy ever offered much explanation for the move — and it was a long one for people then 39 and 35, who had never gone far east of the Mississippi — but it must have been obvious to them that they could not make much of a mark with a private press in Chicago. There might be some advantage in seeking out people who wanted to live the same way and work at the same things.

An antiques dealer whose house was next door to the one they

rented furnished theirs with his overflow and quickly became involved in the unorthodox life of the Goudys, supplying their many and always unexpected guests with ale from pewter tankards and generally taking care of them. To the people of Hingham their life seemed strange. It extended beyond family, for one thing. Soon after the Goudys arrived in Hingham they were joined by W. A. Dwiggins, who had been a student of Goudy's at the School of Illustration and had then worked with him in his Chicago shop on many design commissions. Dwiggins, of course, was to stay on in Hingham and make its name synonymous with great design for decades.

Charles Park, a Unitarian minister in Hingham, who became a lifelong friend of the Goudys, told of their operation:

Their little house was a fascinating combination of home and work-shop. The front parlor was the shop. A small middle room was occupied by Billy Dwiggins, who came a few months later, and still later brought the new Mrs. Billy who proved to be a quiet, gracious little body, always reading. Hingham had never seen people who lived with such zest. They were the soul of friendliness, but had little time to indulge the emotion for its own sake. For them life had a purpose, to create beauty, & to be thorough about it. They threw themselves into their work with a kind of ferocity; laboring, criticizing, cursing mistakes, discussing, speculating, sometimes disagreeing, sometimes exulting, and always with a fierce intensity of idealism that invested life with new meaning for the delighted onlooker.

Mabel Dwiggins — "Mrs. Billy"

Left: Goudy with Mitchell Kennerley
Below: Bruce Rogers, Paul Bennett, and Goudy

— recalled the life of the Goudys in Hingham in less romantic terms, as "a series of waves — crests and troughs." It must have been mostly troughs.

The Village Press did produce nine books while the Goudys lived in Hingham, among them the delightful *Rabbi Ben Ezra* and *Good King Wenceslas*, for which Dwiggins did the decorations. But they could not make a living on the books, and in this remote place Goudy could not get the amount of design work he needed to support the press.

What Hingham did give him that was of value in later years was an introduction to many people in design and printing, including the officers and designers at American Type Founders in Boston. And he became acquainted with Daniel Berkeley Updike and Bruce Rogers. At the time Updike, who was five years older than Goudy, and Rogers, who was five years younger, were both well established in the world of books, Updike as the premier printer in the country and Rogers as the designer and typographer at the Riverside Press.

Rogers had never heard of Goudy when he received a letter from him introducing himself. He later admitted that, on his early visits to Hingham, he was stunned at seeing Goudy cook steaks in the door of the furnace — Rogers was from Indiana but had no experience of the Dakota Territory — but he said, "I liked him at once." Bertha, he felt, did not like him much at first — "perhaps a little jealous of my budding reputation" — but Rogers was to become one of the most loyal friends the Goudys ever had.

In 1906 the Goudys moved to New York City and, with Everett Currier as a partner, set up the Village Press in a Manhattan office building. In his search for work, one of the first people Goudy looked up was Mitchell Kennerley. Kennerley had come to New York from England when he was only about twenty years old to take over the New York operation of a London publisher. His employers often disapproved of his business methods, however, and always of his accounts, and he was soon on his own. He set up his publishing operation in a little office on East 29th Street and very soon made an impression on the publishing world. Kennerley had instinctive good taste, a genius for publicity, and the ability to persuade many of the best printers, designers, and illustrators to work for him. Later he also ran the Anderson Galleries, which put him at the center of the art and auction world. Kennerley sent clients to Goudy, introduced him to publishers, and eventually commissioned him to design and compose books. After his bleak years in Hingham, Goudy began to know something akin to prosperity.

His office was on the twelfth floor of the Parker Building, at 225 Fourth Avenue, on the corner of 19th Street. On the evening of January 10, 1908, the building caught fire and the offices from the second through the twelfth floors were destroyed. Currier summoned Goudy from his apartment on West 117th Street, but the two of them could only stand in the street and watch. Everything in the office was destroyed. Only the matrices for the Village type, which had been stored in the building manager's fireproof safe, survived. A few days later Goudy rented a desk in an advertising office and returned once again to his lettering trade.

He did not, however, leave off designing type. In fact, he had continued to work at it steadily from the time he left Chicago. Between 1903 and the time of the fire he had drawn nine faces, none of them satisfactory to him. Several were done for American Type Founders at the request of Clarence Marder, who had specific notions about which well-known faces he wanted imitated, and it is probable Goudy had little interest in them. He certainly had none in a face he made for the Barron's financial paper in Boston; in later years he could not even recall what it looked like.

Shortly after the fire, the Lanston Monotype Machine Company of Philadelphia asked Goudy to

design a new type for the original *Life* magazine, and he delivered the face that became known as Monotype 38-E, along with its italic. Goudy knew nothing about the monotype machine then, and modifications the company made in his letters, to fit them to the machine, distressed him. In fact, he never did like the type. But printers did, and it spread his name through the printing industry; for many years the specimen books listed it as Goudy Old Style or Goudy Light. The name came from the foundry, not from Goudy, but it was powerful advertising.

His own work in advertising must have been rewarding for in 1909 he was able to make his first trip to England. Since this was a purely professional outing, he was obviously intent on getting back into printing. He visited none of the tourist sites and made no effort to find out about his Scottish ancestors; he went solely to meet printers and students of books. William Morris's associate Emery Walker introduced him to the leading printers and many of the designers in London; to this trip he owed his acquaintance with George W. Jones, the printer and typographer who was to become a dedicated champion of his designs. And Goudy was given something of an education by Alfred W. Pollard of the British Museum, who opened up that library to him and introduced him to other scholars of incunabula. For many years Goudy was able to recall precisely the shape of handwriting and letters in books and manuscripts in the British Museum and to use them as inspiration for his work.

As an education, however, a trip he and his family made to the Continent the next year was more important. In Paris, Milan, Venice, Florence, and Rome their

Top, left: Sir Emery Walker
Top, right: George W. Jones
Above: Fred and Bertha Goudy
with John Johnson, the univer-
sity printer at Oxford

attention was focused entirely on letters, books, paintings, architecture, and design. Their pointed lack of interest in food, political history, and many other things that attract tourists to those places must have made them strange travelers. But they were irrepressible students. In the Louvre Goudy posted Bertha as a lookout to warn him of the approach of guards while he sneaked a rubbing from a block with a Roman inscription on it. Precautions of that kind were not necessary in Rome, where he made rubbings from a number of monuments. But one wonders what officers of museums thought of his drawing letters he found in

Below: Goudy's rubbing of part of the word "Hadriano" from a Roman tablet in the Louvre
Bottom: A showing of Goudy's Hadriano Title, 1912

Renaissance paintings. The effect of that tour on Goudy was immense. Everything he drew afterward reflects its impact on his imagination. He and Bertha made many other trips to Europe in later years, but it was this one that changed his life.

Then he stopped being an amateur of design. At least he said that happened in 1911 when Kennerley asked him to design and set his edition of *The Door in the Wall and Other Stories* by H. G. Wells. Goudy intended at first to use Caslon Old Face, a type designed in the early eighteenth century by William Caslon. But when he saw a couple of trial proof sheets he thought there was excessive variation in color between capitals and lower case letters, as well as too much space between the letters. So he stopped work on the layouts and designed his own type for the book.

A few years earlier Kennerley had brought back from England as a gift for Goudy a limited edition book on the types of the Oxford University Press. Among its illustrations were samples of the type Bishop John Fell of Oxford had bought in the Netherlands in the late seventeenth century. These types, of French origin, were for some decades thought to be the best in England. Goudy decided to use them as a model for his new type, to which he gave Kennerley's name. For the title page of the book and the titles of the stories he designed Forum Title, the name of which reveals its origin: Goudy used as inspiration rubbings and drawings of letters he had made at Trajan's Column and on the Arch of Titus in the Roman Forum.

His production of the Wells book is characteristic of his working habits. He had agreed on a production schedule with Kennerley and the printers, Norman T. A. Munder & Company in Baltimore. Then he delayed initial work on the layouts until he was nearing deadline. He had almost finished the layouts when he saw the disappointing proofs of the Caslon type. He then designed Kennerley Old Style and Forum Title in a single week and had them cut in time to keep to his original schedule. Since it was Bertha who composed the book, she must have borne the most stress in this ordering of work, but if she complained she left no record of it.

Ironically, it was the Caslon Foundry in England that was to make Goudy famous in Great Britain. In 1913 Caslon acquired the British rights to Kennerley Old Style, and the next year it bought five more Goudy faces. The reception of Kennerley in England gave Goudy official eminence. It was highly praised by critics and typographers, including Stanley Morison and Sir Bernard Newdigate. Newdigate wrote that "since the first Caslon began casting type about the year 1724, no such excellent letter has been put within the reach of English printers." The comparison with Caslon may have given Goudy a twinge, but he cannot have been displeased with being raised above not only people like Morris and Ricketts but even above Baskerville.

Two books share the Village Press imprint in 1911. Where the Goudys were working is not certain, although their office address seems to have been Kennerley's. It was 1912 before they were able to rent their own office again, at 132 Madison Avenue, where they installed printing equipment. From then until 1935 the flow of publications from the Village Press is fairly steady.

But increasingly the work of the press fell to Bertha, as Goudy concentrated on new type designs. His reckoning is that between 1912 and 1920 he designed twenty faces.

Six of them, including the still-admired and popular Goudy Old Style, he made for American Type Founders, to whom he was on retainer in 1915 and 1916, before the relationship began to sour.

Among so many designs there were bound to be strange ones. Collier was truly an oddity. Goudy had seen a page in a book printed in 1534 in Switzerland in which the letter d had what he assumed was a damaged serif. Why he would want to propagate this injury is a mystery, but he did, basing the Collier type's serifs on it. He was drawing another alphabet at the same time, for the Sherman type, and he later admitted that he was obsessed with getting a close fitting of letters and "went to extremes."

But that passion for a close fit also led him during this period to

Goudy Lanston, a type in which he solved the problem of the fitting by an adjustment of serifs that he said had been used by the first great printers and then forgotten after the sixteenth century. His output from those years also included Goudy Open and Goudy Modern and its italic, faces that remain popular now.

In 1914 the Goudys moved themselves and their press into a house on Deepdene Road in Forest Hills Gardens, Queens. It may have been nothing more than Goudy's gift for publicity that led him to announce the establishment there of the Village Letter Foundery. (His choice of spelling, which one would have thought current only in Philadelphia at that late date, had an effect; there is much mirth in the print journals of the time

about the "foundery.") Goudy became something of a public figure in Forest Hills. For the next decade he turned up frequently in news accounts of civic celebrations — he was a great promoter of the Fourth of July — and club activities. The house on Deepdene Road became a kind of disorderly salon for all kinds of people involved in design and for people who were not but who liked Goudy's stories. It was here that his reputation as a raconteur was established.

He was becoming a public figure in the larger world as well. From 1915 to 1924 he was an instructor in the Art Students' League in Manhattan, and his students and associates there became the advance troops for making his ideas about design, and his types, known in ever-widening circles outside

the world of printing. For several years after he left the League he held a more imposing teaching post, as professor of design at New York University, but it was really his students from the Art Students' League who carried his gospel out into the streets.

He gave the gospel enduring form. In 1918 he published *The Alphabet* and founded the journal *Ars Typographica. The Alphabet* was first issued under Kennerley's imprint, as was the companion volume, *The Elements of Lettering* (1922). *The Alphabet*, superbly printed by William Edwin Rudge, is a sound instrument for teaching students, printers, and designers. Goudy's discussion of the origins of letters is wholly derivative but quite good. And his arrangement of pages of the letters

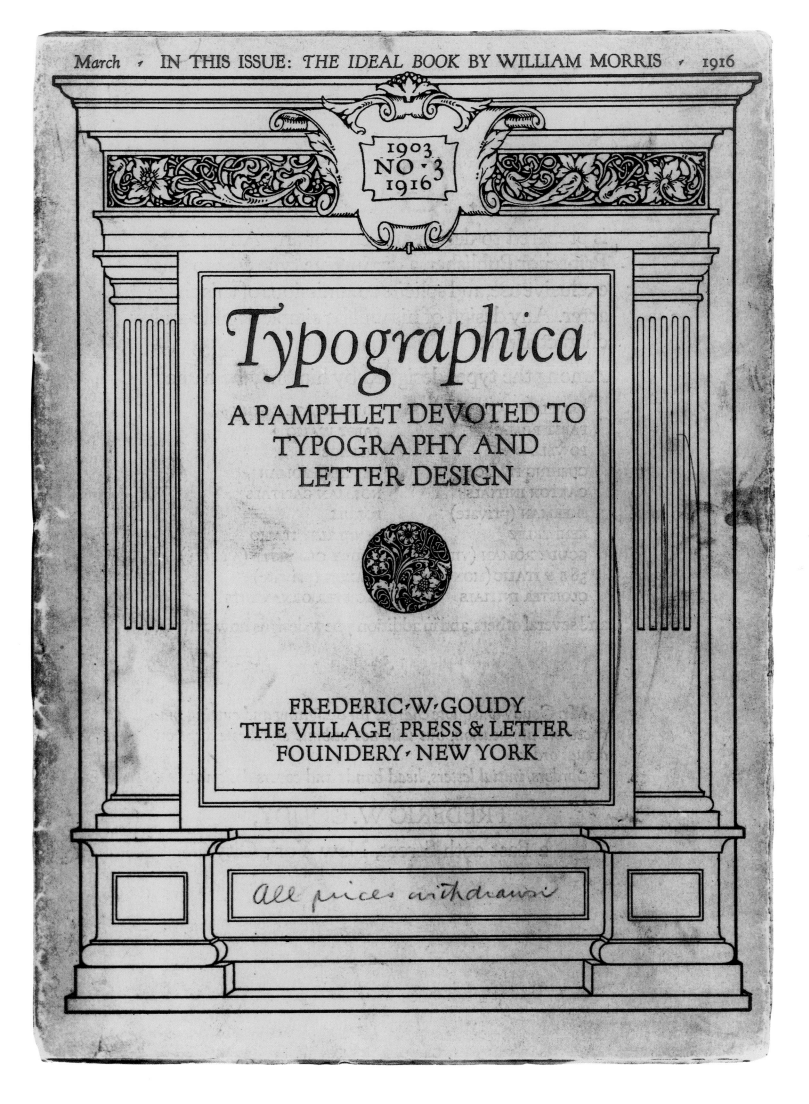

1903
NO · 3
1916

Typographica

A PAMPHLET DEVOTED TO TYPOGRAPHY AND LETTER DESIGN

FREDERIC · W · GOUDY
THE VILLAGE PRESS & LETTER
FOUNDERY · NEW YORK

All prices withdrawn

Set by B M G.

Typographica

NO · FOUR · M·CM·XXVI

◆

A SPECIMEN OF THE TYPES AND BORDERS DESIGNED BY FREDERIC W. GOUDY

ALSO EIGHT TYPES FROM ENGLISH MATRICES

CAST AND FOR SALE BY
FREDERIC AND BERTHA GOUDY
AT THE VILLAGE LETTER FOUNDERY
MARLBOROUGH · ON · HUDSON
NEW YORK

AN INNOVATION IN LETTER FOUNDING

GREAT many printers have frequently wished for a letter which has distinction as well as individuality, and have been unable to find just what they desire among the faces shown by the founderies. To these printers, The VILLAGE PRESS & LETTER FOUNDERY offers the types shown on the following pages. They have been designed by Mr. FREDERIC W. GOUDY, well known as a decorative designer & printer of limited editions. Mr. Goudy's work is in line with the practice of the early printers who, in the absence of type founders, combined letter design and type casting, and having only themselves to please, produced types full of personality. His letters are based on a study of the classic models of the times before printing. They are without eccentricity, and while free from the usual wearying commonplace regularities, yet retain those natural deficiencies and irregularities that give life and character to design.

Mr. Goudy prints only with types of his own design and to do this he has cut matrices at considerable expense. Having these matrices, he has no objection to their use by discriminating printers who are willing to pay for casting and handling. The prices necessarily are higher than those of the type founders, as there is

of the alphabet, in which he gives fifteen forms of each character, all hand drawn, is perfect wordless instruction.

The Elements of Lettering was so harshly caricatured in the *Fleuron* by Stanley Morison that some people have been loath to use it. Actually, it is essential reading for designers and students. Its illustrations of letter forms are at least as interesting as Goudy's analyses of them; the book is a good example of how well Goudy could design when his heart was in the work. The book is also a fine example of generosity; it contains virtually all the information a reader needs to refute its every argument.

Ars Typographica was obviously

Above: "An Innovation in Letter Founding," from Typographica *No. 4*

Opposite: Typographica *No. 4*

inspired by *Typographica*, a journal Goudy began in 1911 and continued for more than twenty-five years, when he felt like it, to promote his own types. *Typographica* is by far the greater piece of design in every number, but Goudy used it relentlessly to promote his own faces. The pages are wonderful to look at. But I would rather admire these pages than read them.

Not all of that apostolic spirit spilled over into *Ars Typographica*. In his hands it was not so much a journal of typography as a vehicle — that is too tame a word; it was a Rolls-Royce or a Hispano-Suiza — for the ideas he wanted to promote. He was a good editor but a domineering writer, who would lecture his readers, especially in his editor's column. He had more than one purpose; Goudy said he meant *Ars Typographica* to appeal to printers most of all. In fact it brought him praise from designers and artists, and from book collectors. It was much commented on in other print journals, but Goudy was nonplussed to find that the printers, in his words, gave "not a damn" about it. Well, it is a bravura performance, and the issues Goudy edited and designed are wonderful to look at.

In 1920 Lanston Monotype named Goudy its art director, and he remained associated with Lanston for twenty-seven years, after 1939 as "art counselor." For a man who was so improvident, the retainer was an assurance. But the job was no sinecure. Lanston specimen books through the 1920s and '30s clearly reflect his influence and taste. And the large correspondence that survives between him and company executives reveals an art director with strong opinions and with a deep knowledge of the company's operations,

especially in its shops (where he did not always win arguments with the feisty type cutters and their foremen). At times he was even a moral force, especially in his efforts to defeat the practice of purloining another company's types.

His position did not require him to design types for Lanston, but by the 1940s Lanston had twenty-nine of his faces, and when he died he left the drawings for one they wanted to issue when he was gone — Goudy Thirty. In his first year with them, he made Garamont, Italian Old Style, and Goudy Newstyle. The first two were made initially for Lanston; the Village Foundery held the rights to Newstyle for a time before Goudy sold it to Lanston.

Garamont was made at the company's request. They wanted a new drawing of the sixteenth-century face associated with the French printer Claude Garamond. Interest in the Garamond types had been revived before World War I in France, and in this country American Type Founders had a Garamond face designed by Morris Benton and T. M. Cleland in 1917, derived from faces used by the seventeenth-century printer Jean Jannon (always regarded as Garamond faces by the French national printing office). The types Goudy modeled his Garamont on are at least partly Jannon, although some of the letters suggest the types in the great Richelieu folio Bible, which were Garamond's own types. In any case, this is the one typeface Goudy produced in which he made a careful effort to copy details of the types he was working from. Lanston then asked him for a new version of Nicolas Jenson's type, but Goudy said he persuaded the company it needed an entirely new type based on Italian Renaissance models, and he gave them

Left: Goudy with members of the Junior Advertising Club of Los Angeles, 1939
Above: Goudy with Mitchell Kennerley
Opposite: Amherst Club dinner, 1939. Among the men at the table are Goudy, Howard Coggeshall, and Bruce Rogers

Italian Old Style. Both faces proved durable in popularity for a long time, and Italian Old Style remains a much-valued type. For both these faces Bruce Rogers made the display sheets. The one for Italian Old Style must be the most glorious display sample of a type ever made in this country. It is hard to imagine that a designer of type could want a greater tribute than it or that he could get one.

By the early 1920s Goudy was being showered with honors, not only by groups concerned with printing and design. Inevitably, some resentment grew up against him, especially among other designers. That feeling was largely silent when he was given the Gold Medal of the American Institute of Graphic Arts in 1920, but when the American Institute of Architecture reached outside its pre-

cincts and gave him *its* Gold Medal in 1922, some of the ill will found its way into print. Eventually there developed a kind of running battle between people who were for Goudy and those against him, and at times it became mean.

It was also very often tainted by motives that could at least be questioned. One of the leading critics of Goudy, who questioned the originality of his designs and even his standards, was Henry Lewis Bullen, a man whose taste and scholarship assured that what he said was taken very seriously. Bullen was also the director of the American Type Founders library and museum. Goudy had parted company with A.T.F. in the years before 1920, not altogether pleasantly. A.T.F. had added several of its own shop designers' faces to Goudy Old Style and packaged

the lot of them in advertisements and offerings as the "Goudy Family." Goudy's reaction to this invasion was a little intemperate — and he never got rid of his annoyance about the matter — but it was not loud and not really unreasonable.

In any case, the opposition to Goudy among the printers and designers coalesced around Bullen for a few years. In general, what was said was that Goudy was always designing the same face and giving it new names or copying ancient ones and giving them his name, or that his origins in advertising made him suspect, or that he simply had not the learning of some others in the profession who had nothing like his fame. In general, the response of Goudy's supporters was to raise the level of publicity about him and the

praise of him. Reading the public pronouncements made by or about Goudy in the 1920s, one has to keep in mind that controversy lay behind them, and, since most of the criticism of him was not published, it is necessary always to figure out what inspired any sudden burst of admiration.

Goudy's conduct in all this will stand the test of probity better than that of his opponents on the whole. Bullen, for instance, went on pressing his case against Goudy as late as 1930, when both men were growing old. But when Bullen died in 1939, Goudy gave a rather wonderful talk at his memorial service about how much he owed to Bullen's library and to the man.

Such a delicious feud could not be contained within American borders. In fairly sharp and

useful form it turns up in correspondence between Daniel Berkeley Updike and Stanley Morison in 1923 and 1924.[11] The letters are good summaries in some ways. The tone and dimension of the dispute are clearly revealed in a letter Morison had received from an American, part of which he quoted to Updike. Frederic Warde, a designer and typographer who had fine academic credentials and connections, was utterly unknown to Morison when Warde wrote him a letter. By this time Morison had become touchy about Goudy, and presumably Warde knew it. Warde's letter lampooned the behavior of the Goudyites, and Morison excerpted a bit of it for Updike:

...you would not have been quite at home at the recent celebration, jubilee, medal-pinning orgy with wh. the more audible

bander-log of this land indicated that they were proud of Mr. Goudy. It was very loud & very long & it may be that they chanted

> *Goudyamus igitur; and*
> *rend the air with cheers;*
> *Juvenem dum sumus: for*
> *discretion comes with*
> *years.*

Warde's sarcasm is no more revealing than Morison's glee at the passage, including the juvenile macaronics.

The exchange between Updike and Morison leaves one with the impression that the great printer was inclined to court the favor of his younger correspondent by feeding his rancor; so it is hard to know how to take some of his remarks about Goudy here since in his later years he was very generous in his appreciation of Goudy types. In this case it was Updike

who had brought up the subject of Goudy, innocently enough. He had sent Morison some samples of Garamont and asked whether it was the same face then being issued by the English Monotype Company as Garamond.

Morison exploded. He was associated with the English Monotype Company, and he wrote back that their version was much superior to Goudy's. In fact, he added, he himself had suggested that Monotype cut the type. He was furious with Goudy for using his own name in association with the faces he made, and he expressed real revulsion: "I shudder to think of the terrible things that Mr. Goudy now threatens to do. I suppose he will do a Blado italic — and call it Goudy. I must get ahead first. But I thank God, there is something else in printing besides type-

faces & swash characters!" Goudy was proud of the swash characters he had made for the face, but Morison felt sure the "ugly swash" characters attributed to Garamond, on which Goudy had based his, were not Garamond's at all. Finally, what Goudy had done with his Garamond, Morison said, was "reproduce the letter he found" at the end of F. A. Duprat's *Histoire de l'Imprimerie Imperiale de France.*

That is catty, but Morison knew his man. Goudy had been most extravagantly praised in American journals for imagined innovations and changes in the Garamond face when he had changed it less than any other original he based a type on. And Morison was generally right about the origins of the letters Goudy produced. What gives his malice away is his

worry about a forthcoming Goudy Blado. In an advertisement issued shortly before this letter was written, Goudy had said the Village Press could set type in Blado, a type based on the face cut by the Renaissance Roman calligrapher Lodovico degli Arrighi, usually called Blado after the printer Antonio Blado. Goudy never said he was designing such a type. Morison was being a little paranoid.

Later in the Morison-Updike exchange Updike advised Morison not to "flatter Goudy by including him" in a survey of American designers he was arranging for the *Fleuron*. Updike added that "on the other hand I would be tempted, when you tell me the

truth would be told, because it would be such fun to have the truth told for once in that quarter!"

This exchange of letters contains the main criticism of Goudy heard even now. Morison assumes at one point that Goudy has a public relations man working for him. Often now one hears that Goudy himself was a mere public relations man. Morison's annoyance at Goudy's name appearing on his types must spring from his perception that it was a kind of claim. From the early age of printing down through the centuries, printers had given the names of very famous people to types, names of printers or designers or, some-

times, of authors of books in which the type was first used. It might strike the fastidious as unseemly for a modern designer to name them for himself. But, of course, the foundries were the first to apply Goudy's name to some of his types, and while it came to appear on twenty of them, he made almost a hundred that are not called Goudy.

Neither Morison nor Updike invented these complaints. The value of them lies in their appearance in letters concerned with many other things; in casual remarks people use what is current. In a sense Goudy was the victim of his own success. He had preached good design and did more than anyone else to create a large public for

the debate about taste in print at the very time when design was becoming a respectable subject for academics and intellectuals. As the group of the interested grew, it began to divide, and some people in it knew they knew more than others. Goudy was far too democratic to know anything of the kind. He would give talks about his ideas to anyone, and he loved applause. His personality was the agent for the popular acceptance of many of his ideas, and it was the cause of most of the resentments against him. For some reason Americans do not like to admit that the purpose of a club is to keep people out, and the usefulness of snobbery is exclusion. That

Above: The house at Deepdene, Marlboro-on-Hudson, March 1948
Left: Fred and Bertha Goudy in the workshop at Deepdene, October 1933
Right: Goudy inking type
Opposite: Goudy's workshop at Deepdene

principle holds even when the snob is right, and in the fight over Goudy the critics were often right. That a few were unfair is beside the point. As long as he lived Goudy had his revenge; there was nothing vindictive about him, and his habit of seeking solace by inspiring more praise drove his opponents to new heights of fury.

There was a regional aspect to all of this, too. Peter Bielenson referred to that when he wrote that Goudy was "an erstwhile bookkeeper from the mid-West, who had risen from the ranks by virtue of taste and skill." Bruce Rogers summed it up best, in an open letter to Goudy in 1938:

There is a certain rugged di-rectness in your attack on a book problem that somehow I connect with your favorite bill-of-fare of those earlier days when I first knew you. When we were invited to dinner at your house... I knew the chances were ten to one that we would sit down to a thick porter-house steak (perhaps broiled through the furnace door) and mashed potatoes....You were all for the noble (albeit expensive) simplicity of diet; and I think there must be some hitherto un-traced connection between steak-and-potatoes and type design. For one of the last and most skillful American punch cutters, John Cum-ming of Worcester, who cut the Montaigne type, always gave me steak and potatoes when I vis-ited him....

The great distinction between you and most other type design-ers of the present day is that you, as a printer, can, and frequently do, use the types that you pro-duce. And this ability gives you an enormous advantage over the other designers; for I feel sure that when (as you describe the process) you think of a letter and then draw a line round it, you are thinking of it not only in relation to all the other letters in a word, but also of all the words as a page, and of all the pages as a book—even to the binding that is eventually to enclose it. It would perhaps be hard to prove, but I think that thus keeping the ulti-mate use in mind subtly influences your power as a designer.[12]

At the time all these feuds were started, in the 1920s, Goudy was young enough — he was approaching sixty — to take some delight in them. In later years he became somewhat bitter, although he never mentioned individuals.

In 1923 Goudy began looking for a place where he could do all his work, not only designing and printing but cutting matrices and making fonts. His old friend Robert Wiebking of Chicago, who had cut all of Goudy's matrices from the beginning, was dying, and Goudy decided he was too old and too much a perfectionist to

Views of the mill at Deepdene
The ink drawing is by Charles
E. Pont, August 16, 1939

seek out another man who could satisfy his demands in type cutting.

He found an old house and an adjoining mill at Marlboro-on-Hudson, on the west bank of the river about seventy-five miles north of the city, bought it, and moved there in 1924. He and Bertha gave it the name of their street in Forest Hills, Deepdene. In the mill they installed the heavy equipment, and on the upper floor, actually the entry floor, they set up a shop for designing, composing, and matrix cutting. The mill's little waterfall became a figure in some of the Village Press books and the object of some fun in satirical or comic verses Goudy's friends wrote about him in later years.

During one of his trips to England Goudy had seen a machine made for engraving matrices, which had been fabricated in Germany. It operated like a reverse pantograph and reminded him of a panto-

graph he had bought for a quarter when he was a boy. After he moved to Deepdene he went to Germany to visit the Stempel printworks, found the manufacturer of the machine, and had one built, with some modifications he specified.

At that time he was drawing letters seven and a half inches high. The machine allowed him to cut metal patterns one-third the size of the drawings with a stylus that controlled the cutting tool producing the metal pattern. Tracing the metal pattern, he could then engrave the types with a tiny drill that was guided by the edges of the pattern. The ratios could be adjusted so that any size of type could be cut. It was while he was working on the machine that Goudy noticed that at some time he had lost the use of his right eye. When I first read his own account of this and then those of others, I was not very ready to accept them, but since I have found from con-

versations with opthalmologists many cases in which vision has disappeared from an eye without the seer being aware of it. In spite of his dilatory habits — or perhaps symptomatic of them — Goudy was a driven man who paid not a lot of attention to himself; he seemed to regard his body as part of the landscape. When he was trying to sharpen his grinding tool under a microscope he suddenly discovered he could not see through the right eye, and that vision never returned.

Goudy was sixty years old when he began engraving matrices, and after that he cast all his types and sold them directly. The fifty faces he made after that include some of his most interesting — the Deepdene types, Goudy Text, Goethe, Village No. 2, the Trajan inscriptional face, and some calligraphic ones. He even made one for a typewriter. And after the matrix-cutting machine had been destroyed

*Below: Fred and Bertha Goudy
on the porch at Deepdene
Opposite: Goudy and his son
Frederic in the workshop at
Deepdene*

in a fire, he went on designing types, the last a Hebrew face for the Hebrew University in Jerusalem.

For the purposes of this book, the story of Goudy's life in his last twenty-two years is in those type-faces. But he did much more than make drawings. His travels and speeches increased enormously. He and Bertha took to driving great distances for his speaking tours. In 1925 they drove to southern California, where Goudy was beginning to develop a large network of friends. He took many assignments to conduct seminars in universities from Virginia to California and accepted almost any excuse to deliver a speech, especially in New York. There are still

people around who can recall the old man on his visits to the city, sitting with one or another friend behind the New York Public Library on 42nd Street, indulging in their favorite pastime, girl watching. His good eye was good to a great age.

Bertha Goudy settled into Deepdene in a way Goudy could never settle into any one place. Their son and his wife, Alice, had jobs in the family enterprise, and Bertha presided over the whole of it. She mastered the matrix-cutting machine soon after it was set up and began cutting matrices just as she had long been setting type. There is no disagreement among people who knew her that she was the one who kept the Village Press

running through its long life (it is one of the longest-lived private presses in history). Its record is impressive. In thirty-five years, it produced more than one hundred and sixty books of various sizes and more than seventy-five broadsides, pamphlets, and other fugitive pieces, a number of these smaller pieces of considerable value for their design and printing. Strictly speaking, all the productions of the Village Press were limited editions, but some books were issued in six hundred or eight hundred copies. Some of the fugitive pieces, on the other hand, were done in single copies as presentations for friends.

Bruce Rogers said Bertha was the fastest compositor he had ever

known—"and the best." Scores of testimonies from printers and designers validate that judgment. She came to her mastery more slowly than many have said. In 1911 when she was setting *The Door in the Wall* under deadline pressure she made mistakes that can be seen easily. By the middle of the decade the mistakes are gone from Village Press books, and after that anyone can see on her pages the work of a master of composition. It was not as a mere compliment to her that Rogers had her set his edition of his letters exchanged with T. E. Lawrence. It is a lovely book.

Her son said that in some ways, especially in her willingness to enter into an argument over ideas,

Bertha seemed more a Goudy than his father did. Rogers confirmed that opinion, saying that Bertha "was quick at everything, and quick-tempered." Frederic T. Goudy's brief evocation of the family's ways, with people inventing a reason for an argument rather than letting wits go slack, sounds as though the house became unbearably interesting at times.

Being the only son of the two Goudys cannot have been easy. When Frederic T. was middle-aged his father was writing him, on hotel stationery, from California instructing him about printing and also about how to build a new matrix-cutting machine (the letter includes drawings of parts of the machine). Young Fred seems to get lost in the shadow of his parents, and he finally disappears altogether from the record within a decade of his father's death. He left little written down about his mother, but some interesting thoughts about his father. If he was resentful he never said so, but in a pamphlet addressed to Goudy in 1938, as part of the thirty-fifth anniversary of the Village Press, there are a couple of telling paragraphs from the son about the father:

I remember how greatly, when I was a small boy, you puzzled me. Other boys had fathers who went to work a few hours a day and after that they had lots of time with their sons. You worked harder than any of those fathers, and longer. Days, nights, weekends, and holidays you were always busy and yet we seldom had time or money to do lots of things our neighbors did. I blamed you for that because no one ever explained to me the difference between a man building a career for himself on his own, and one who drew a regular pay envelope....

Well, much water has gone over the dam here at Deepdene and many Goudy typefaces have flooded the world since those far-off days when you used to tap my penny bank for carfare.[13]

If there were notes of discord at Deepdene that were audible to visitors, they had little to do with personal feelings. The place was in a general uproar. Since Bertha was often unwilling to interrupt her work, guests became accustomed to dinners made in ten minutes with whatever was to hand — sometimes, as Rogers said, with meat cooked in the furnace. Some groups of visitors, if they threatened to bother Goudy for long, found themselves taken by Bertha on long nature walks next to

the Hudson. She was a considerable gardener and could tell them the names of every plant they saw, and those of the birds.

Birds were her specialty. She kept a large aviary, most of it in a caged-off section of the porch of her house, where some birds were kept in separate cages and others flew free. There were other animals as well. It had always been so. Will Ransom recalled that when he and Goudy started the Village Press in Chicago there were dogs, cats, and one Goudy child underfoot constantly in their print shop in the barn. He also recalled that when they had worked late in the barn and the light was gone, they would haul everything into the dining room of the Goudys' house

and distribute the type there.

At Deepdene Bruce Rogers counted two parrots and twenty-nine other birds, two Newfoundland hounds, a small black terrier, a horse, and a cow. He failed to notice the pride of cats roaming the place. Paul Bennett wrote: "This may sound as though the Goudys maintained a small zoo — there was an outdoor pool with fish, too — but to me it seemed something less, say a modest menagerie of tame creatures who squawked, screeched, and growled." George Macy, founder of the Limited Editions Club, said the birds were "all very beautiful, and they stank. One, a large black low-flying fellow, plooped on my shoulder. Another, a small and dazzlingly scarlet bird, settled affectionately in my hair, and a whole bottle of tar soap failed that evening to remove the evidence of his bird-like affection."

Visitors were also expected to drown out squawk, screech, and growl with singing. Bertha had a trained contralto voice and was a good pianist. Mabel Dwiggins laughed over the memory of Bertha's inveigling staid Hingham women into rousing versions of show songs. At Deepdene singing was part of the routine.

Goudy looked as though he fitted into this environment easily. His friend Howard Coggeshall, the noted printer, has a description of Goudy at home:

He liked to dress well, though never expensively, when "off the range." Around the shop he was wont to appear in some pretty nondescript outfits — usually old knickers which he preferred up to within a few years of his death. Though neat and immaculately attired when away from Deepdene, his domestic appearance often shocked the home folks and caused

Below: "A Tribute to B.M.G.,"
broadside set in Bertham
Opposite: Bertha composing
type

*the visiting delegates to specu-
late and wonder.*[14]

"Delegate" is a neat word for the Deepdene pilgrims.

Goudy was a nut for machines and gadgets, not only the machines he kept in the mill for his work, but automobiles. Coggeshall says he "kept himself broke" buying them. Among them was a magnificent old Cord. At different times he was a pack rat for all sorts of things. Coggeshall recalled most vividly the razors: "His assortment of safety razors was the most extensive in the Western Hemisphere. If he heard of a new make that he did not possess, he was pretty sure to step right out and buy himself a copy." The razors seem innocent enough, but hardly the cars. However, no one says anything about the safety of the roads around Marlboro-on-Hudson when they were traveled by hot cars in the hands of a man with one good eye.

It may have been out of a sense of competition with him that Bertha took to collecting. Her daughter-in-law, Alice, said Bertha fretted about attending a celebratory dinner one night, saying she would have to wear earrings and she thought she would look silly in them. Told she looked fine, she began a collection of jewelry that eventually included more than two hundred pairs of earrings, even a pair that belonged to the Empress Josephine. It is comforting to think of someone as accomplished and as workmanlike as Bertha Goudy going to Paris to buy Josephine's earrings.

Bertha was a consummate craftsman. In the last year of her life she was ill almost constantly, but during that time she set the type for the Limited Editions Club *Rip Van Winkle*, and it is a superb piece of work. She died at Deepdene

A TRIBUTE TO B·M·G

❖

THESE lines present my one-hundredth type design [yet unnamed] before lining, fitting, or final revision. The type, drawn in humility, is dedicated to the memory of my beloved helpmate

BERTHA M· GOUDY

She encouraged me when my own courage faltered; uncomplaining she endured the privations & vicissitudes of our early companionship; her intelligent and ready counsel I welcomed & valued ; her consummate craftsmanship made possible many difficult undertakings ; she ever sought to minimize any exploitation of her own great attainments, that the acclaim which rightfully was hers should come, instead, to me. For two-score years, in every way, she unselfishly aided me in my work in the fields of type design and typography & enabled me to attain a measure of success which I could not have achieved without her.   F·W·G·

Marlboro, June, 1936

on October 21, 1935, when she was sixty-six years old. In many ways Goudy never recovered from the loss of his best friend. Two years after her death her women friends in printing, who belonged to a group known as "The Distaff Side," asked Goudy to write a booklet about her. It is the most awkward, even painful, thing he ever wrote; it seems nearly choked. And when it comes to an account of her work, it stops. "When asked to write a few words about her as a printer," Goudy wrote, "I find it a most difficult task." He then simply quotes Paul Bennett's opinion.

For several years after Bertha's death, it seems to anyone looking through the Goudy files that every moment not given to designing types must have been occupied with dinners given in Goudy's honor by friends bent on keeping him in good cheer. The greatest celebration was a tremendous series of events in honor of the thirty-fifth anniversary of the Village Press in 1938, with many publications issued in tribute and fetes given in New York City as well as at Deepdene — enough to provide grist for Frederic Warde's mill for a lifetime, one would have thought. The printed tributes and declara-

tions of affection came from people ranging from printers' organizations to members of President Roosevelt's cabinet. Some bandarlog. Among those testifying was Daniel Berkeley Updike.

The general celebration that filled those years was so noisy, in fact, that it generated a number of roastings of Goudy by his admirers, among them a dinner given by the Society of Printers in Boston in 1937 at which Goudy was awarded two "degrees"— T.D.P. (Type Designer Prolific) and R.E. (Raconteur Extraordinary). Anyone interested in the tone of the badinage that was meant to delight Goudy should look at some of the poems and broadsides produced by his friend Earl Emmons, another editor of *The American Printer*, who shared Goudy's taste for hoi polloi and pranks. Emmons — whose literary works include *The Ballad of Mae West's Bust* and *Reward of Virtue*, a versified version of *Diamond Lil*, both of which deserve resurrection in an anthology — ridiculed Goudy's hat in a long poem. When Goudy was interviewed on network radio by the most popular newsman of the day, Lowell Thomas, Emmons printed the text in a wild little book called *Hello everybody! This is Goudy speaking. Now friends, we bring you that great star of the radio, screen, and graphic arts, Frederic W. Goudy in person.* Goudy was not incapable of lampooning himself in similar ways. A very good example concerns his favorite piece of propaganda, a little sermon on the importance of type called *The Type Speaks*, first issued in 1931 and sent out again in several different formats and in different typefaces through the years. All but one begin: "I am type!" The ringer starts with "I am tight!"

VI : The Story of a Type

I AM ASKED so frequently how I begin a new type, where I get my inspiration [if "inspiration" is not too important a word in this connection], and very often why I use this form or that rather than another, that I believe the story of the type used herein will illustrate concretely the matters, covered generally in the rest of this book, which relate to the type designer's problems. It is the story of an actual commission to design a type, and it suggests, too, the thousand and one mental quirks and turns, "the various moods of mind that through the soul come thronging," so difficult to recall, but very real in the process of bringing a new type to life, and varying with every new essay. The story serves also to fix definitely the matter of its provenance [a matter of some interest to me, since I find that already in my own lifetime some of my early designs are credited to others], and this account is therefore of bibliograhic interest.

In my library in a bookcase where I keep the books which interest me as possessing special typographical details, or as products of private presses, or as typographic curiosa, rather than for any literary quality they may have in them, I found recently [while I was looking for another book] a copy of John Milton's *Comus and Other Poems*, published in 1906 by the Cambridge University Press and printed in a hodgepodge of incongruous types. And the thought occurred to me that no university with a university press, so far as I could recall, possessed a type which had been designed for its exclusive use, and I could not help wondering why the head of some great university had not

[47]

PABST ITALIC
[Design No. 6]

Not long afterward, in 1903, the American Type Founders Company commissioned me to draw an italic to accompany the Pabst Roman, and this I did. I remember particularly the interest I took in watching the making of the patterns for this type by Robert Wiebking, who engraved the matrices for the foundry. As it was a letter characterized by a freedom of outline which followed my hand lettering, he had considerable difficulty in preserving the subtle ins and outs of my freehand drawing without undue exaggeration of them. I remember also that the foundry paid me $100. for the design, an unheard-of figure for a type design in those days.

ABCDEFGHIJKL MNOPQRSTUV WXYZabcdefghijklm nopqrstuvwxyzABDG MNPRTQu&$£fifffl fffffi?!';:-'.1234567890

54

POWELL
[Design No. 7]

About the time of cutting the Pabst Italic, Powell left Schlesinger & Mayer to become advertising manager for Mandel Brothers, another large department store. Still type-minded, he asked if I would design a type for his advertising there. Of course, it must be different from Pabst, and yet have the same quality of freedom and spontaneity. Some years before this, as I have told on an earlier page, I had hand-lettered for W. W. Denslow the verses of *Mother Goose*, which Mr. Denslow had illustrated. This letter was distinctive and unlike anything in use in those days. I have also told how it attracted the attention of the Inland Type Foundry of St. Louis, who, without bothering to acquire rights of reproduction, made it into type, and—horror of horrors—named it "Hearst"! The main features of that letter were the short ascenders and descenders with high middles, that is, such lower-case letters as

ABCDEFGHIJKLM NOPQRSTUVW XYZ&ÆŒ.,';:!?- abcdefghijklmno pqrstuvwxyzæœ fifffl$1234567890£

55

Of the types Goudy designed in those years the one he was most tender about was his memorial to Bertha, the face called Bertham, done in 1936. But by far the most successful was the University of California Old Style, a classical face that was much used. The first correspondence about this type dates from 1936, when a trustee of the university asked whether Goudy would consider making a face for the university press's exclusive use. Goudy wrote a fine

account of the genesis of the type in his book *Typologia*, published by the University of California Press. The matrices were cut by Lanston, and the letters in that dossier between Goudy and Sol Hess of Lanston about the specifics of the cutting make a fine education.

In 1939 Goudy was devastated by a second fire. In the early morning hours of January 26, he was awakened, whether by light or the sound of someone shouting from

across the river is unclear. When he looked out his window, he saw the mill blazing. The efforts of firemen from several communities to contain the fire were useless, and the entire structure and all its contents were destroyed. All the types, the matrices for scores of them, most of his drawings and patterns, virtually the entire record of the transactions of the Village Press and the type foundry, and a great deal more, were lost. A few patterns for letters in the

Goudy collection of the Library of Congress are singed, indicating he did pick up some things from the debris, but on the whole the only things he had left were odd pieces he had kept in his house.

The fire was a news event, different accounts of it appearing for more than a month afterward in papers and magazines, along with editorials, profiles, and columns. Printing associations on both coasts and in the Middle West raised money to help Goudy out.

The Advertising Club in New York appealed for contributions, and there are boxes of notes from people on Madison Avenue sending five-dollar and ten-dollar donations. Two years later Goudy was still answering mail he received within weeks of the fire. His letters reveal a resigned attitude. In many he gives vivid descriptions of what he saw and did and sometimes detailed lists of things lost in the blaze, but his comments indicate he saw it as a kind of natural act that he regretted but felt no personal remorse about. A few years later the University of Syracuse bought a matrix-engraving machine for its printing school and put it at Goudy's disposal for the rest of his life.

The fire made him eventually decide to sell his collection of personal records, and many books, to the Library of Congress. Whether he needed the money or simply feared that some other disaster might destroy them is not clear. But he took several years during the 1940s arranging them, and in 1946 the library put on a large show of his work.

As would happen so often in his last years, the people who suggested new work to Goudy after the fire were Californians. The University of California Press asked him to set down his ideas about design and types, and he delivered the manuscript of *Typologia* to it in 1940 and then worked on the design of the book. He then revised *The Alphabet* and *Elements of Lettering* (both of which had been issued in limited numbers) and combined the two in a single volume, which the University of California Press published in 1942.

He also went to California to lecture in two different years at Scripps College, and it was his

Lost Goudy Types
[1939]

THE TYPES and ornaments used in printing this booklet were all designed by Frederic W. Goudy and all represent faces that were lost—drawings, patterns and matrices—in the disastrous fire which totally destroyed Mr. Goudy's Village Press at Marlborough, N.Y., in the early morning of January 26th, 1939. The types are:

TRAJAN 1930
Goudy Newstyle 1921
Goudy Tory 1936
Bertham 1936
Kaatskill 1929
Mediaeval 1930
Goudy Friar 1937

With the exception of small fonts in a limited number of composing rooms throughout the country, these types are gone forever.   H.C.

Above: "Lost Goudy Types," broadside printed by Howard Coggeshall in 1941 and set in Village No. 2
Opposite: Goudy

association with the students there, who wanted a type of their own from which they could learn printing and composing, that led him to design the Scripps roman and italic faces. His health remained good through most of the years of the Second World War and he traveled west quite often, a couple of times to see his sister in Oregon but mostly to events or talks organized by friends like the Grabhorns in California.

Beginning in 1943 Goudy recorded in his letters a number of illnesses that kept him from working for weeks or even months. But he and Emmons worked together on a complete compilation of his type designs, and by the end of 1944 Goudy had also finished writing the elegant little two-vol-

ume account of his types printed by Typophiles, *A Half-Century of Type Design and Typography, 1895-1945.*

Goudy died in bed at home, of a heart attack, on May 11, 1947, and was buried next to Bertha in Evergreen Cemetery in Chicago. He was memorialized in hundreds of editorial pages in this country and in England. A sentence in the editorial in the *New York Herald Tribune* on May 13 summarizes what most said: "The entire reading public is in Mr. Goudy's debt."

He had thousands of friends — all those people he wrote to constantly — and the Goudy files in several collections are filled with letters written about him after he died. There are more eloquent ones than that written, presumably to Paul Bennett, by Arthur Rushmore of the Golden Hind Press in Madison, New Jersey, on May 13, but Rushmore's has the emotion and even the exaggerations that are common to most:

Goudy knew what he wanted to do and he did it. Starting from scratch, late in life; self-taught, creating his own techniques, haunted by the spectre of want; he went his own sweet way and without fuss or fanfare built a record of achievement in the graphic arts that will outlive the granite dedicated to conquering heroes. Books persist, ideas cannot be burned, and as long as civilized thought continues much of it will be read in the characters that Goudy drew and cut and which other men throughout the world, unheeding, have set and printed.... He was often in want, more often than not because of his simple belief that all men were honest and fair. He was no businessman, he did not want to be. He found it easier to be a gentleman, and more comfortable.[15]

Goudy was a printer for more than forty years, a typographer longer than that; he had designed magazines and book covers before he had any clear notions of typography, and his original art was lettering. His experience in all these occupations was undoubtedly critical to his esthetics and judgments about his later work as a type designer. During his life it was not uncommon for his partisans to extend their admiration for his types to everything else he did, and some arguments against his types and his ideas about type design owe more than a little to resentment against those claims. If Goudy had chosen to make his living only as a printer, a letterer, a designer of magazines or books, or a typographer, he would not be remembered now. He was good enough at all those professions, sometimes very good, but he set no standards for any of them; his own humorous testimony about the indifference of printers to *Ars Typographica* tells the whole story. He became a great force in the movement to raise standards of printing and typography, but his power rested on the acceptance of his types; he was able to use that to promote a larger general debate about standards. To put his

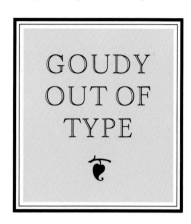

GOUDY OUT OF TYPE

position in perspective, one has only to ask whether he ought to be compared with Updike, among his contemporaries, as a printer, or with a few private printers since Updike who have far exceeded even that man's performance. And in typography, would one compare Goudy with Bruce Rogers or with Dwiggins?

Could Goudy have been unaware of such comparisons and judgments? That is not likely. He was a very smart man about the business of life. And that intelligence has to be taken into account when one considers his eventual decision to concentrate on type designing to the virtual exclusion of other work. Goudy always assumed he could do anything he wanted to, and his energy was indeed prodigious to a great age. If he had felt strongly about his contributions to book design, printing, typography, or even lettering, he would have worked harder at those tasks.

In general, Goudy had a much sharper eye for a good page than for a sequence of pages and a sharper sense of what is required to show off a stanza of poetry than a page of prose. He was a better designer of magazines than of books, but even in the magazine

Below: A decorated letter drawn by Goudy for The Door in the Wall
Opposite: Title page of The Door in the Wall *from a prospectus Goudy prepared for the edition. This marked the first use of Kennerley*

THE DOOR
IN THE WALL
And Other Stories

BY

H·G·WELLS

ILLUSTRATED
WITH PHOTOGRAVURES FROM
PHOTOGRAPHS BY

ALVIN LANGDON COBURN

NEW YORK & LONDON
MITCHELL KENNERLEY
M C M X I

Song. CHLORIS FAREWELL

PHYLLIS! *why fhould we delay*
Pleafures fhorter than the day?
Could we (which we never can!)
Stretch our lives beyond their fpan;
Beauty like a fhadow flies,
And our youth before us dies.
Or would youth, and beauty, flay,
Love hath wings, and will away.
Love hath fwifter wings than time:
Change in love to Heav'n does climb;
Gods, that never change their ftate,
Vary oft their love and hate.
PHYLLIS! *to this truth we owe*
All the love betwixt us two:
Let not you and I enquire,
What has been our paft defire:
On what fhepherds you have fmil'd,

[9]

format he was comfortable only with the design of individual issues; he had no eye for a design that might serve fifty-two or five hundred and twenty issues. Among his most striking conceptions were advertisements (for which he also did his best lettering), and his most impressive pieces of design and printing are broadsides, not unrelated to advertisements. His interest in all those things declined rapidly after he was sixty, when he began to engrave his own matrices and became the king of type.

It is ironic that Mitchell Kennerley intended to start Goudy off on a career in the world of big book publishing in 1911. The result was Goudy's rather sudden rise to fame as a type designer. As a piece of book design, *The Door in the Wall and Other Stories* by H. G. Wells, done by Goudy for Kennerley, is a fairly subtle production. But it shows Goudy's limitations at least as clearly as it shows his strengths. It compares favorably with the best work of the crowd of designers and printers that fol-

Above: Pages from the 1911 Village Press edition of Songs and Verses Selected From the Works of Edmund Waller, Esq. *Opposite: Goudy's setting for "Le Bonheur de ce monde," a sonnet by the sixteenth century Antwerp printer Christoph Plantin*

lowed William Morris.

The titles, initials, and decorations are inspired and the pages on which they appear are very beautiful; what is characteristic of Goudy is that they have a strength that is rare in other examples of such deliberately artistic productions. To be sure, the individual pages of the entire book are pleasurable. Goudy placed a body of type about seven and a half by nine inches on an eleven-by-fourteen-inch page with wider margins at the outside of the page and

LE BONHEUR
DE CE MONDE

SONNET
Compofé par Chriftoph Plantin

AVoir une maifon commode, propre & belle,
Un jardin tapiffé, d'efpaliers odorans,
Des fruits, d'excellent vin, peu de train, peu d'enfans,
Poffeder feul fans bruit une femme fidéle.

N'avoir dettes, amour, ni procés, ni querelle,
Ni de partage à faire avecque fes parens,
Se contenter de peu, n'efpérer rien des Grands,
Régler tous fes deffeins fur un jufte modéle.

Vivre avecque franchife & fans ambition,
S'adonner fans fcrupule à la dévotion,
Domter fes paffions, les rendre obéiffantes

Conferver l'efprit libre, & le jugement fort,
Dire fon Chapelet en cultivant fes entes,
C'eft attendre chez foi bien doucement la mort.

under the body; at first glance the pages suggest the framed look of engravings in late Renaissance volumes. Goudy may have wanted to harmonize the pages of type with those that had photogravures made from photographs by Alvin Langdon Coburn that were interleaved throughout the book. If he did, that was a mistake. Virtually every page looks exactly like every other, without any of the fine variations a more practiced or imaginative typographer would have introduced to keep the eye from tiring. The monotony is not bothersome if one is reading only one story at a time, but *The Door in the Wall* is a difficult book to read right through. Its rhythms are all confined to the pages and keep repeating themselves pages after page.

As a display piece for the Kennerley type the book is as good as Goudy could want. That face was very widely used for decades, and it does not really appear to better advantage anywhere. But in compelling attention to the type the book also invites a close look at the printing and the composition, which are the most striking features of its manufacture. They were not Goudy's. The compositor was Bertha Goudy, and the printing was done, albeit under Goudy's supervision, by the printers in the shop of Norman Munder in Baltimore.

The proper comparison to be made with *The Door in the Wall*, for the purposes of design, is the Village Press edition of *Songs and Verses Selected from the Works of Edmund Waller, Esq.*, which was also produced in 1911. Everything about that little volume of verse is classy. Goudy chose an italic face, and an italic is exactly right for the civil, light, cavalier sensibility of Waller. Goudy's page de-

Below and opposite: Title page and opening page of The Alphabet

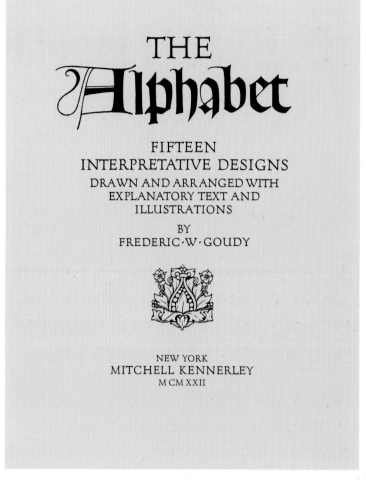

signs are triumphant. It is enough to make one wish Kennerley had hired Goudy not for the Wells book but for an anthology of poetry. In the Waller volume Goudy's hand is so sure and his delight in varying the visual rhythms throughout the book so evident that his inspiration might have gone for hundreds of pages without repetition. This book is a good example of Goudy's printing. As it should do, the tactile quality of the page comes first to the eye, even before one is tempted to run fingers over it.

Indeed, among the Village Press productions, the books or pamphlets of poetry are superior to all others. Goudy's masterpiece in this genre is a broadside of "Le Bonheur de ce monde," a sonnet by Christoph Plantin. Considering the sonneteer's place in the history of printing, Goudy meant it as a tribute to typography and printing, and it is a fine one.

Among the books of prose Goudy designed, *The Alphabet* and *Elements of Lettering* are the most satisfactory. That is hardly surprising; in both he was dealing, in a way of his own choosing, with a problem that always gave him pleasure — how to illustrate. The text he wrote for both books argues in different ways around his illustrations of letters and typefaces. He might have been more fanciful in the design of some pages — he tended to block off illustrations too regularly — but on the whole he provided easy access to fairly complicated information in a natural flow that allows the reader's memory and

imagination to build on what he has seen, from beginning to end. Critics of Goudy's tight packing of type, and those who think his pages always look too dense, ought to have another look at these books. He opened up the pages and gave them a kind of grandeur. There is a lesson in leading here that is well worth learning.

The one disappointment is the chapter of notes preceding the beautiful pages illustrating letters in *The Alphabet*. Goudy had to provide full accounts of the fifteen different shapes of letters that appear on each of the pages of his alphabet. He could not put all of that on one page, and he certainly could not repeat it on all pages. But by placing all the explanatory information in one chapter before the alphabet illustrations, he asked the reader to memorize too much too quickly. And, for those who cannot remember, leafing back and forth from the alphabet to the notes can be annoying. Some of the Renaissance books Goudy studied for their types are masterpieces of typographical semiotics; they make enormously complicated material available on a page, and available to the memory from page to page, with magisterial authority. Perhaps if Goudy had had the languages of those books he might have picked up hints from them about how to approach the problem he faced in *The Alphabet*.

Nonetheless, these two thin volumes are fine examples of book design. Some designers working for large publishing houses have since learned more about how to handle difficult information more efficiently than Goudy could have imagined, but Goudy had some strange and charming notions of arrangement of type in such situations that are worth study.

By the time he came to design

The Alphabet

Chapter I. *What Letters Are*

 LETTER is a symbol, with a definite shape & significance, indicating a single sound or combination of sounds, and providing a means, through grouping, for the *visible* expression of words—that is, of thoughts. Originally, letters were adaptations of natural forms employed in picture-writing, but by a process of evolution, [actually degradation,] they have become arbitrary signs with little resemblance to the symbols from which they are derived. These arbitrary shapes have passed through their periods of uncertainty and change; they have a long history and manifold associations; they are classics, and should not be tampered with, except within limits that just discretion may allow.

An ornamental form once found is repeated, the eye grows accustomed to it and expects its recurrence; it becomes established by use; it may be associated with fundamental ideas of life and nature and is handed on and on, until finally its origin and meaning are, perhaps, lost. Just so, the pictorial significance of individual letters is so deeply buried in oblivion that special study and research would be necessary to resurrect their original form or meaning—an undertaking not essential here.

Language itself, as an organized system, was of necessity slow in developing; the next steps, the approaches toward a more or less phonetic alphabet, were equally lingering; for speech existed long before it was discovered that the human voice could be represented by symbols—thus

[9]

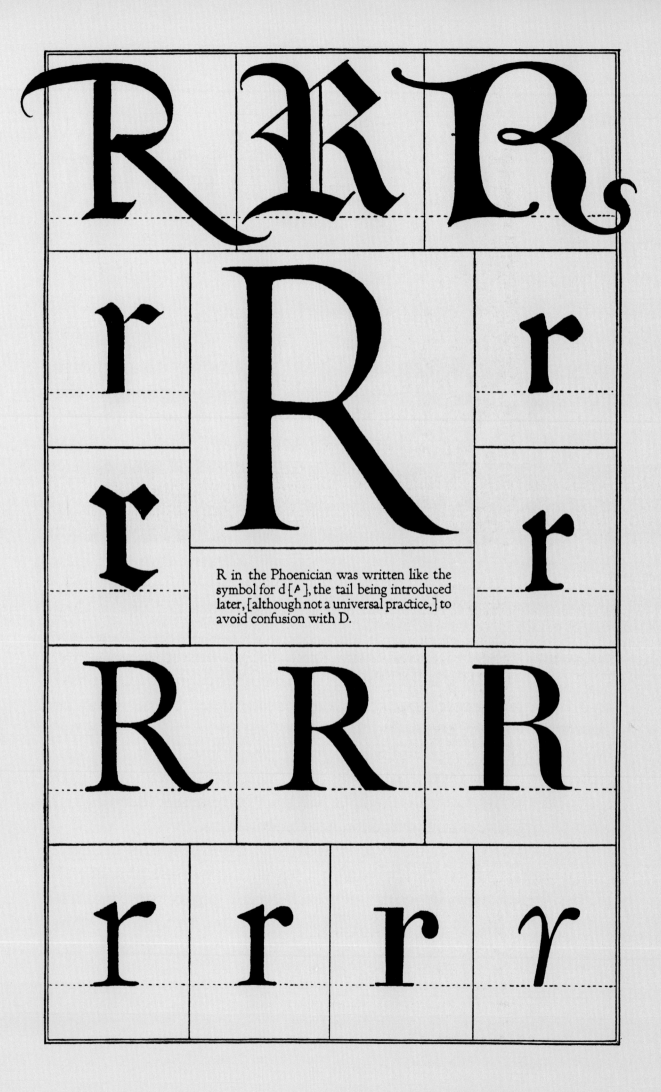

R in the Phoenician was written like the symbol for d [ᴀ], the tail being introduced later, [although not a universal practice,] to avoid confusion with D.

BEAUTY
IS THE VISIBLE
EXPRESSION
OF MAN'S
PLEASURE IN
LABOR
C D G J K Q
W Z &

FIG. 11 'FORUM' CAPITALS BY F.W.G. [1911]

THE ROMAN CAPITAL

one of the Tripods at Thebes, both practically contemporary with [39] the Sigean fragment, read from left to right only. The letters are cut on a pillar of white marble, nine feet high, two feet wide, and eight inches thick, which quite probably supported a bust or statue of Hermocrates, whose name appears in the text of the inscription. The writing itself presents a specimen nearly three thousand years old.

In the British Museum there is a brass signet, found near Rome, the appearance of which indicates very great age. The signet probably was intended for stamping or printing its owner's signature on documents that were written on parchment or other substance used for receiving writing. On its face, which is about two inches in length and four-fifths of an inch wide, letters of good proportion [in reverse] are engraved in relief within a border line or rim. A ring, which serves as a handle, is attached to the back of the plate. The letters are capitals huddled together with little punctuation, in the usual style of the old Roman inscriptions. They spell "CICAECILI HERMIAS.SN.," or, as we would print it today, "C.J.CAECILI HERMIAE SIGNUM," which translated is, "The seal of Caius Julius Caecilius Hermias." Of

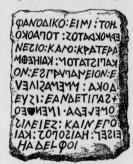

FIG. 12 SIGEAN TABLET, ILLUSTRATING BOUSTROPHEDON

[TRANSLATION]
I am Hermocrates, the son of Phanodicus, of this Promontory, and I have presented in the Prytaneum a cup with a stand and wine strainer, as a monument to Sigeans. If, then, on any account I am troubled, I go to the Sigeans, and Aesopus, and my brethren have erected this monument for me.

his own *Typologia* for the University of California Press twenty years later, Goudy had lost much of his instinct for that type of design work. How much is difficult to judge. Goudy acknowledged the cooperation of Samuel Farquhar, manager of the press, and the contributions of old collaborators are difficult to sort out. Goudy was not a man to resign his prerogatives, however, so it is not unfair to charge him with the results. *Typologia* is a lot of fun to read. Goudy was confident, and even more unbuttoned than usual, when he wrote it. But the design is undistinguished and there are places where Goudy did not choose good

Above: Pages from The Alphabet and Elements of Lettering
Opposite: Goudy's drawings of the principal forms of the letter R from The Alphabet

sites for illustration of the types he wrote about. A reader inevitably makes dog-ears in pages for easy referral. The four pages illustrating the designs for the University of California Old Style typeface, in which the book is printed, are singularly ill placed. In fact, given his overall subject, a lifetime's observation about the design of type, Goudy should have resisted the temptation to use that face; he had designed others that would have been much more suitable. There is one bit of unintended entertainment in the book, however — the chapter on fine printing, which is very wise and will quickly teach the reader to

point out the flaws in the book he is reading.

As with all of Goudy's books, the most single pleasing page of *Typologia* is the title page; one can almost feel his enjoyment in designing it. That is true of many of his best cover and title page designs. Unfortunately, it is also true of some of his annoying ones. The place where his personal enjoyment gives least pleasure in this book is on the first page of the text, where Goudy drew an initial M for the first paragraph that is downright offensive; in size, color, and shape it is out of harmony with everything else on the page.

In general the smaller books

Goudy designed and printed for the Village Press are good productions, but it is hard to think of any one would choose to include in a display of the very best work done by private presses in the last hundred years. The most impressive productions of the press, in fact, are booklets or leaflets that gave Goudy a chance to show off his own types. One, done in 1915, *A Note on Letter-Design and the Village Types*, is a tour de force of illustrations of types and borders. He could do that sort of thing very well with a more regular text, too, as he did in *Three Essays* by Augustine Birrell, a book that is a fine display of the Goudy Newstyle typeface.

Many broadsides issued from the Village Press through the years, some of them meant to display new typefaces; some were poems, some had texts of well-known documents like the Gettysburg Address. Probably the perfect Goudy page is a broadside of 1915 called *Ellen Terry at the Neighborhood Playhouse — An Appreciation*. Its combination of exuberance, indeed wild energy in places, restraint, and above all its humor make it thoroughly delightful. There is a lot of the sly and commanding spirit of a grand old actress in it. That, of course, makes it the perfect Goudy page in the bad sense of the term. It shows off too grandly.

Goudy worked on magazine designs for more than forty years and a few of them are spectacular. He had drawn covers for many in his first years in Chicago, but it was his work on setting and printing *The Chap-Book* that changed his imagination about magazines. He was entirely responsible for the early issues in the four-and-a-half-by-eight inch format. The issues are uniform enough to announce

themselves as versions of the same magazine, but they contain an immense variety of conception. Will Bradley's initial work on the covers — usually done entirely in red and black boxed lettering on white paper — faithfully predicts the contents. The production of the drawings and decorations, text pages and announcements, is distinctive and the little magazines are sometimes surprising, often beautiful. Few publications of that age that are so obviously meant to trumpet the beauties of Art Nouveau are as satisfying.

Much more familiar are two later magazines — *Ars Typographica* and the five numbers of *Typographica*. The latter was an occasional journal issued by the Village Press to display Goudy's types and often to promote his arguments about design, lettering, readability, and anything else that was on his mind. In terms of design, *Typographica* is the more successful. Since everything in it was by Goudy, presumably he could tailor the content to his own design if he had to. However it was done, the result is good. Except for the first issue, the numbers seem to have been designed as wholes, not just collections of pages. The visual rhythms are precise, unpredictable, and inevitable. Of course, the very perfection of *Typographica* makes it a bad model for a magazine of more general interest. There are far too many unusual features in these designs to make them imitable. But they are eloquent testimony to Goudy's ability to imagine a single, powerful, and beautiful shape for a large body of printed material.

The four numbers of *Ars Typographica* produced under Goudy's hand are in some ways more indicative of his skills as an editor than as a designer. The articles

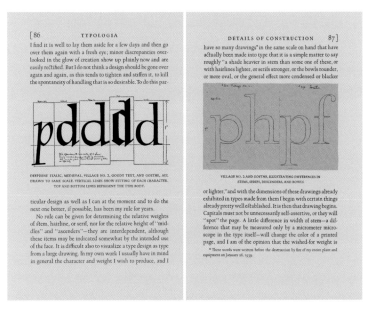

Above and opposite: Pages from Typologia

and other items are ingeniously chosen and placed to leave the impression that the journal had a definite political statement to make — within the politics of the design world. In all of them Goudy had an "Editor's Workshop" at the back in which he could scatter his obiter dicta and scold or cajole. But otherwise he was usually only one among other authors. In Number One he had articles by Holbrook Jackson on the revival of fine printing, Gertrude Burford Rawlings on Aldus, William Blades on the early schools of

Typologia

STUDIES IN TYPE DESIGN & TYPE MAKING

WITH COMMENTS ON THE INVENTION OF

TYPOGRAPHY · THE FIRST TYPES

LEGIBILITY AND FINE

PRINTING

FREDERIC W. GOUDY, L.H.D., LITT.D.

∴

BERKELEY AND LOS ANGELES

UNIVERSITY OF CALIFORNIA PRESS

1940

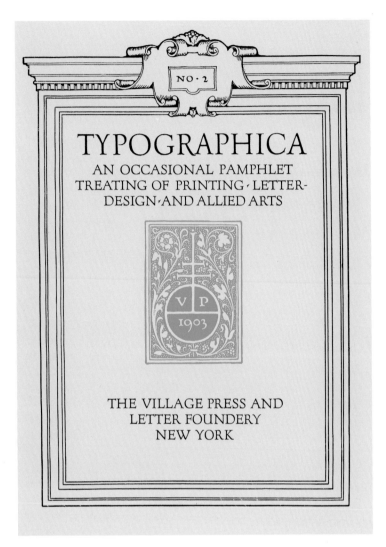

and another by Charles Ricketts on woodcuts in the fifteenth and sixteenth centuries. Typography was the subject of the third number, with two articles by Goudy, on handpress printing and "printing as an art," and a very knowing one by Talbot Baines Reed on fashions in typography. That number also contains the original version of the Plantin sonnet magnificently set in Garamond type. Goudy's last issue was done many years later, in the autumn of 1934, and is obviously a tribute to his wife. Virtually all the material is by Goudy, and it is set in seven of his typefaces. The endnote tells why he did it: Bertha had actually begun to set the pages but had to stop because of a "serious illness," and someone else completed the work. Bertha was never to work again. Within a year she was dead.

Visually *Ars Typographica* is often too monumental. That may be one reason why printers at the time ignored it. The pages are magnificent, but they resemble great slabs of inscriptions. As often happens when Goudy sets out to overwhelm the reader, one finds oneself looking closely at the composition and decoration first. Goudy was not achieving his own first goal — readability.

For more than twenty-five years, from the early 1890s, Goudy designed covers, first for books and then for many kinds of magazines. He proudly preserved his early book covers but made no special claims for them, and they really deserve none. They are pleasant and, as was characteristic of Goudy's early work, notably uncluttered, but they are very much of the period. Some of the magazine covers are memorable. Designing them was an art Goudy learned by trial and error, but he learned well. He probably made more covers for

The Inland Printer than for any other magazine, and it is instructive to go through them in order. One of 1898 is a very messy affair that might have been turned out by overworked advertising departments of stores at the time. Its one relieving bit of humor is the inclusion of the price ridiculously in the banner of the coat of arms that has its own pretentious humor. By 1900 Goudy's control, his sense of neatness and spareness, had improved markedly. And in the July 1901 issue he reached a standard that set his work apart and remains striking now. That issue has the added interest of a drawing of a monk acting as a scribe. It is in the center of the cover and is probably Dwiggins's first published drawing.

What Goudy was learning in *The Inland Printer* jobs was simplicity. Later he would return to some very elaborate designs that are orderly and beautiful, like the fine decorative cover of *The Chicago Literary Club Yearbook, 1911–12.* He had made some very good cover designs for such different periodicals as *Brentano's Book Chat*, an occasional literary magazine, and *Interior Decoration.* Goudy also designed the covers for Kennerley's magazine, *The Forum*, and as late as August 1919, he designed a cover for *Art and Life.* All these jobs are quite creditable, and they demonstrate that Goudy had not lost, well into upper middle age, his ability to learn, from himself as well as others. In the third decade of this century it would have been impossible for him to make a living as a designer of covers at all, unless he had been willing to dedicate his life to that work. Magazines were beginning to turn over the entire job of design to their own people, whether in-house or in outside shops, and

typography, Goudy himself on type design in history and in the present, and A. W. Dow on the educational work of the American Institute of Graphic Arts. The second issue was dedicated to the graphic arts more widely conceived. It is notable for some very handsome illustrations of engravings and woodcuts and has a remarkable Bruce Rogers design of an illustrated page in the style of the eighteenth century. Its articles include a long one drawn from an encyclopedia on the work of William Bulmer and the Shakespeare Press, one from a history of engraving on Thomas Bewick and his followers, one by Edward Strange on decorative title pages,

Above: Typographica *No. 2*
Opposite: Ars Typographica, *Autumn 1934*

VOL 1 N 4   AUTUMN, 1934   RUME MB

Ars Typographica

FREDERIC W. GOUDY EDITOR

THE PRESS OF THE WOOLLY WHALE

NEW YORK CITY

VOL 1 N 4   AUTUMN, 1934   RUME MB

Price, 25 cents

The Inland Printer

PAN-AMERICAN NUMBER

JULY 1901

THE INLAND PRINTER COMPANY
CHICAGO AND NEW YORK

the design of periodicals was itself becoming one of the most important commercial aspects of the publications.

What Goudy liked best was the challenge of one occasion. Given the chance to design a cover for the magazine published by Taylor and Taylor in San Francisco, *T & T Imprint*, in the winter of 1917, he produced a knockout. Of course, that publication was made for printers, and Goudy had some teasing fun in the design of his cover. But he had versatility, too. He cannot have had much interest in the content of *The Annals of Medical History*, but he designed good monumental covers for it in 1917 and 1922; they may

be more stately than warm, but they are surely as imposing as the doctors could have wanted them to be.

Goudy's first design work was in advertising, and the earliest examples of it are simply lost. They certainly exist somewhere, in the files of newspapers in some library, but since he kept no record of payments or those records were destroyed in one of his fires, it becomes impossible to trace them. There is no reason to doubt the testimony of his contemporaries, however, that they were notable for their cleanliness and order. If one wants to see a later example of what his eye could do, there is a Peerless automobile advertisement

by him in the files of the Library of Congress that would do credit to a demiminimalist of our own times; it gives Peerless all the blatant attention the company could want without making the reader feel he is being drubbed into paying attention. The lettering is not, perhaps, as fine as that Goudy did for Filene's department store in Boston in roughly the same era, but it is worth some patient study for what it tells one of Goudy's types. Altogether too much has been made by critics who have never even set type, much less designed it, of the effect of his expertise as a letterer on the shapes of his type designs. In fact, he overcame his first profession too successfully in some

of his late typefaces, as in the University of California Old Style, but by now students ought to be able to sit back and look at his lettering for what it is, without prejudice.

I am not sure how much one would learn by tracking down all of his advertising work. A few very good examples will immediately tell that he had a classical and traditionalist sensibility from the beginning and that he favored type so overwhelming against illustration that his dedication to letters cannot be doubted. And the few examples one finds now of his lettering in advertising are so superior as to suppress doubts about his mastery.

"We shall have to set new standards of aesthetics when photomechanical typesetting replaces present methods," Goudy told an interviewer for *PM* magazine in April 1935. It was significant that Goudy volunteered the remark. For several years before, in lectures and in seminars at universities, he had been talking approvingly of different new technologies. From the beginning of his career he had no fear of machines and had resolutely maintained that so long as a machine was used by a designer, compositor, or printer as a tool and nothing more, it was a desirable instrument. By the 1930s some of his peers were beginning to agree, but through the two previous decades he had been abused a good deal for his defense of machines in the production of type. At different times he had publicly contradicted the most respected authorities, including Rudolf Koch, Stanley Morison, and Daniel Berkeley Updike. Bruce Rogers wrote a pamphlet in the '20s generally endorsing Goudy's main arguments, and later W. A. Dwiggins was to enter the fray on his side. But even his defenders were often a little behind him. His remark about photomechanical typesetting, and his willingness to rethink esthetics in connection with new systems, struck many in the world of print as distasteful.

The history of the craft was against him. For several centuries after the first movable types were first used, all type was made by hand by a method which gave type its distinct appearance. A metal punch of each letter was made by a punch cutter and then driven into a brass plate to make a matrix. Once the walls of the matrix were carved or filed clean and the impression was cut to the desired depth, type was made from hot metal poured into the matrix. The compositor hand-set the type in a stick and inserted bits of metal between letters and words to get the line of type desired. Everything was determined by the judgment of the eye. Once a page of type was set, it was secured into the chase by quoins and the chase was locked into the press; then the press was operated by hand.

The steam engine changed all that, making machine-driven punches, mechanical typesetting, and mechanical printing possible —

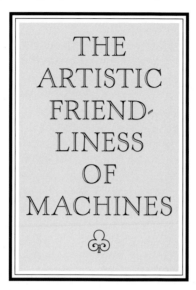

THE ARTISTIC FRIEND-LINESS OF MACHINES

Goudy working with his pantographic matrix-cutting machine

about four centuries after Gutenberg. It is useful to remember that Goudy was twenty years old when the Monotype machine became available. On the whole, the advent of mechanical printing was not a great blessing. Esthetic standards declined precipitately in the nineteenth century. Typefaces became increasingly bizarre, typography was all but forgotten, and the quality of paper declined even more rapidly. Those were the conditions that gave rise to the movement of William Morris and his friends to restore order, clarity, and beauty in printing. The more they and their successors studied the old types and the old books, the more dissatisfied they became with what was being produced. Eventually Koch, Updike, Morison, and many others began to say that what was most needed in design was a return to punch cutting if type was ever to regain anything of the individuality and character it had in the beginning, and some insisted on a return to the entire array of old methods of producing books and making paper.

Their arguments were not unfounded and can be extended even further now. With the triumph of what Goudy called photomechanical typesetting, typefaces have been increasingly denuded of individuality. A comparison of even the best-made books now with the best commercial productions of the 1920s and '30s will quickly reveal how uniformity has made most printing a dull affair. The rise of illiteracy is hardly surprising; the wonder is that anyone reads at all. And the situation is worse in newspapers and magazines. Designers have resorted to startling arrangements to overcome the dullness of the text.

Goudy was very traditional in the matter of esthetics. That vir-

tually all his successful types were old style faces is not incidental. But he did insist that, since most of what people read was being produced from the outset by machines, the conscientious designer had to work with the machines. He himself published scores of books in limited editions that were entirely handmade, but he knew most printing could not be done that luxuriously. His argument was a moral one, that the best people in the craft ought to be involved in making mass production esthetically better. In that sense he was an ally of Peter Behrens and not of William Morris.

His sometimes incautious remarks about the necessity of mastering the machinery rather than letting the machinery master the user reveal a certain contempt for people who feared the effect of the machines. That attitude, as much as anything he said, got him into trouble with his peers, and sometimes with the makers of the machines, the printers, and the foundry men. For more than thirty years he had frequent fights with shop workers at American Type Founders and Lanston Monotype about their execution of his designs, fights that were only intensified by his own mastery of the machines they used. When he was surprised by modifications made in the letters of the first face he made for Lanston, to fit them to the machine, he learned not only how to operate a Monotype machine but how the entire mechanism was designed. When the Remington company asked him to design a face for its typewriters, he made the same kind of intricate study of that machine. His notes indicate he understood in great detail its complex action, including the arcs made by the typing arms as they rose from their

Goudy in his workshop

bed and struck the paper, the effect of the ribbon on the impression produced, and the problems of arranging proper spacing between letters raised on bodies that were necessarily uniform in size. Not that all his study made him any more welcome at Remington than he was at the foundries; one supervisor told him that he and his men did not need Goudy to tell them how to design type for typewriters.

After 1925, of course, he also used machinery, which had been modified to his specifications, to make all his own matrices and types. And it was fairly common for his critics to make his friendliness for machines part of their strictures on his designs. In *Typologia*, as he looked back over his career, he wrote that "the only impeccable designers are those who have never designed a type." So much for the critics. As for the others, his argument is worth quoting at some length:

The practice of any craft should be governed by common sense, and I mean here to refer to purely technical considerations rather than to speak of any aesthetic qualities that are presented by the work in hand. You put your mind to it, you round your back to the burden of inevitable mistakes, and sooner or later you achieve the end desired. You do your best with tools which aid but which do not lessen the manhood of the user. I do not believe that it is the use of a machine or of machine tools that makes a thing bad — it is the evil use of them. Used as a tool, the machine minimizes labor which is necessary but which, in itself, is merely painful and monotonous. The most complicated mechanical device is justifiable if it aids good design or improves the qual-

ity of the product for which it is employed, but not if it helps to make machines of our souls.

In Part X of The Colophon, *a book collectors' quarterly, the late Rudolf Koch, one of Germany's outstanding type designers, wrote: "The engraving machine is seeking to displace craftsmanship, and we must bring pressure to bear in opposition." Theoretically I am in agreement with his statement, but I feel that some qualifications are necessary in relation to certain facts which he does not bring into the picture. I cannot bring myself to regard handicraft as so*

circumscribed as he presents it. Why continue Nicholas Jenson's slow and painstaking methods of producing types — methods which were necessary in his day because he did not possess the instruments of precision available today? As well return to the tallow dip for our lighting or to the slow stagecoach for transportation....

Rudolf Koch wrote also that, "It can be said that unquestionably the character of the old good types comes from the punch. This is the plastic basis of type-cutting; since it is impossible even

with the greatest care to make the form of the punch exact, as much more often, even with long experience, variations occur, the result of counter-punching is always a surprise to the type-cutter. Often the result can not be saved and the punch must be replaced by another; often, though, it can remain, even though it falls short of expectations, if one has freedom enough to make good use of the result. Such forced variations can come, in the hands of an able punch-cutter, to a very beautiful result." Can it be that the beautiful types of the past are due to

*Below, left: Goudy inspecting
the matrix-cutter under a microscope
Below, right: The matrix-cutter
grinder*

*Below, left: Goudy inspecting
the matrix-cutter under a microscope
Below, right: The matrix-cutter
grinder*

*mere accidents of punch-cutting?
I am inclined to think that Professor Koch was speaking more
particularly of his own achievements than of punch-cutting in
general.*

Goudy was seldom so deft in
flicking away the objections of the
rigid.

Too much has been written
about the machinery Goudy used
in his own manufacture of types
without much attempt to understand what he was doing and, as
far as I can tell, without any attempt to duplicate his methods in
order to test them. His chapters

on pattern making and matrix engraving in *Typologia* will explain
the method very well to anyone
who is patient and willing to run a
few simple tests. Goudy's machines
reduced his seven-and-a-half-inch
drawings of letters, first to a two-
and-a-half-inch metal pattern and
then to the type size he wanted.
An often repeated criticism of his
types is that his large drawings
did not reflect a good handwriting so much as a lettering hand,
and this tendency was accentuated by the machines. Anyone can
test that proposition for himself
by drawing very large letters de-

rived from a good manuscript hand
and then reducing them photographically to a standard type size
and comparing them with the
original hand they were based on.
He will quickly find that the shape
of the letters has nothing to do
with the size of the drawings. That
test is simpleminded, perhaps, but
so was much of the criticism.

Suppose his drawings were good
by anyone's standards. It is often
suggested that in some way his
machines removed some of the
character or idiosyncrasies of the
original designs. Given the microscopic accuracy of the measure-

ments made by the machines, that
is unlikely if not absurd. Goudy's
pattern-cutting machine, an elaborated pantograph, was made for
him in Munich according to his
specifications. His comments on
it in *Typologia* make it clear that
it would reproduce every accident
of the large patterns made from
his drawings with the kind of
precision one would expect from
the finest tools. The matrix-engraving machine, also modeled on
a pantograph, was a modified form
of the standard matrix engraver
developed from the models made
by Lynn Boyd Benton. These machines are no longer commonly
made, but one can find examples
of them, and it is worthwhile to
search one out to get some insight
into the criticisms often made of
Goudy's types.

A common statement about
them is that Goudy could never
produce a truly straight or angled
corner since his cutting tools were
rounded points. That evaluation
ignores a couple of things. First,
all types not produced by driven
punches were made by methods
that slightly changed the sharp
angles in any drawing or conception of the letters. Second, Goudy's
cutting heads were ground fine
enough to produce matrices that
would have errors of not more
than two thousandths of an inch.
Some of his cutting points were
ground down to within twenty or
twenty-five ten-thousandths of an
inch — that in a day when standard Monotype matrices allowed
a tolerance of error of up to two
hundredths of an inch.

Under a strong microscope anyone can see the minute rounding
of angles in Goudy's own types.
His proof sheets, in fact, will show
it under a microscope. But in faces
of less than twenty points not even
an ordinary magnifying glass will

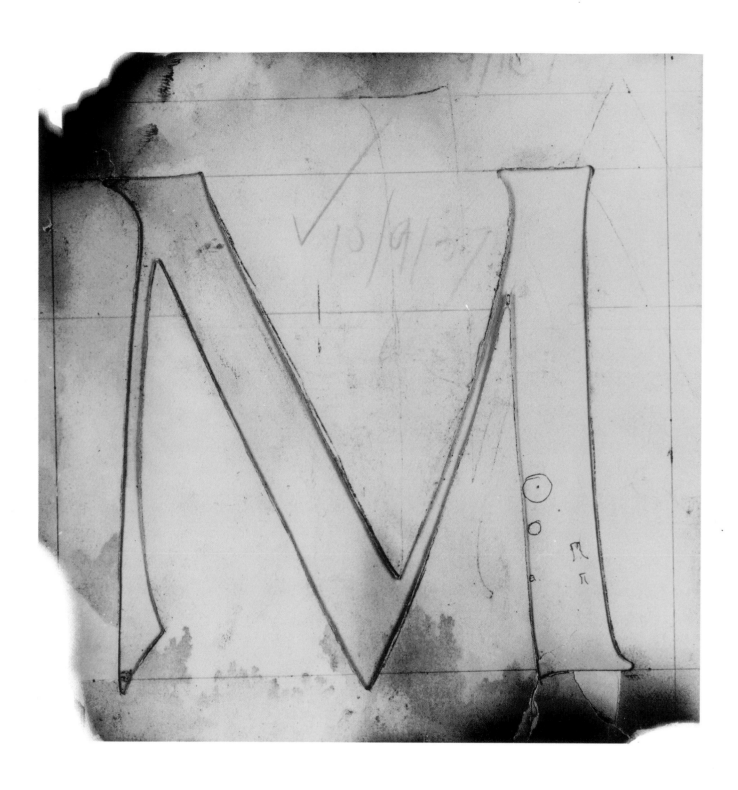

Above: Pencil rubbing and tracing of Friar capital M
Right: Goudy cutting a letter pattern
Opposite: Pattern for Friar capital M, dated October 9, 1937, singed by the fire at Deepdene

reveal the slight impression of the tiny ball point of the engraver, and it takes a very clear eye in bright light to guess at it in the larger sizes.

As to the criticism that his machine tools gave too clean a finish to the edges of his types, it is true that a comparison of his types with those of the earliest designers will show a much cleaner finish along the edges of letters. But he wanted them to, and I think most readers would agree with him. In fact, the best handwriting of the scribes, on which the earliest punch cutters based their designs, shows that same cleanliness of line. Too many commentators have not taken the time and trouble to look at good, old manuscript hands and compare them with the earliest types and then with modern ones, or they have not bothered to decide what the standard ought to be. Goudy's standard is at least definitely stated

by him and defensible.

By now the question of a standard is not academic. In the digitized type generation, designers will have to deal philosophically, in terms of esthetics, with that question. Many typographers now assume that resolutions of over two-thousand lines per inch cause the unacceptable raggedness on the edges of digitized type to disappear and that it is possible to produce clean new faces easily. But if they think about the size of the pixels that form digitized type and then consider the size of Goudy's cutting tools, they will realize that they will need tremendously greater resolutions to get the kind of precision he was producing fifty years ago. Eventually they will. And eventually computer programs that allow instant type designing will force every typographer to face the same esthetic questions Goudy was constantly discussing.

There is reason to think he

would have loved to stay around long enough to see these developments. He was sixty-one years old when he began performing all the steps for making his own types; he was seventy when he teased the *PM* interviewer with his remark about esthetics and photographic methods of type making; when he was eighty he was still writing new arguments for experimenting with new methods. Like Cervantes, he preferred the romance of the road; he had little interest in the inn. A man that cranky and determined would not even have had much hesitation, one would guess, about taking on the computer companies and making their faces more readable — on the screen and on the printing machines.

Some of Goudy's pronouncements on esthetic standards are amateurish, but they kept improving right into his ninth decade. A Goudy now would find a way to

lay down some ground rules for the new generation of everyman type designers that would guide them along the lines of tradition. For Goudy had, in Sir Jacob Epstein's phrase, very public brains, and he was a most traditional man. At the moment his traditionalism is what ought to be emphasized. But that he would have encouraged every new voyager is clear enough from his own statement:

The important point is to know where the handwork should end and the machine work begin, and especially to see that the facility of the machine does not tend to usurp or displace any of the functions of creation and representation. The appearance of the work itself is of more importance than any quibble over the method of its translation into the vehicle of thought, since its legibility or beauty is determined by the eye and not by the means employed to produce the type.

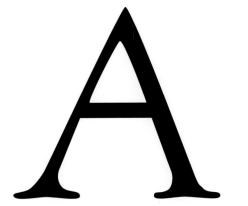

Kennerley Old Style

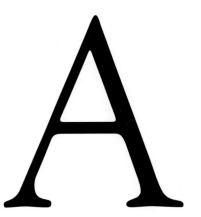

Goudy Old Style

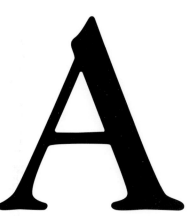

Goudy Modern

Garamont

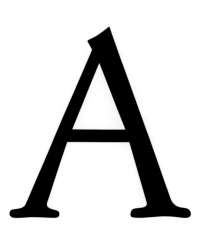

Goudy Newstyle

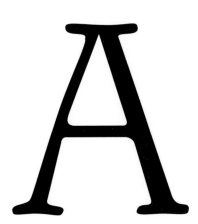

Italian Old Style

Saks Goudy

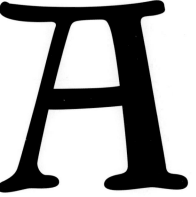

Mediaeval

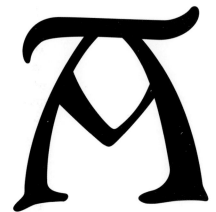

Franciscan

An annotated list of all the Goudy types follows, but I thought it useful to supply some particular comments on some of the faces. In part, this section is confessional, in that I want readers to know what my comments on the types in the annotated list and elsewhere mean – to me, at least. I am not a professional designer or printer and I have found through the years that the vocabulary of type design is maddeningly imprecise, even confused. I am not the person to define terms for the profession and am not even certain that definition at this time would be useful. The comments on the nine faces here, along with those on Deepdene at the beginning of the book, will provide, I hope, terms of reference to clarify my own ideas without twisting Goudy's notions of esthetics.

NINE
FACES,
MANY
FAMILIES

❖

The typefaces in this section are not necessarily those I think are among Goudy's best. In fact, that is an argument I would like to avoid. It is best left to printers and designers. But the types discussed here should allow a reader to make connections with other Goudy faces in a way that will let him network connections among the whole body of Goudy's work. If he does, he should then be able to make connections between Goudy's work and many other bodies of lettering, writing, and type designing. At least I hope so. But the conversation I have tried to enter into this book is one which has been interrupted for so long that some disconnections must be expected.

That there is great variety in Goudy's work is obvious, and that variety is the cause of a good deal of the rejection of his work among contemporary designers. That their rejection is wrong is the argument of this book. Here I would simply invite some reflection on what the craftsman was up to.

Kennerley

This 1911 design had a fine debut in England. Sir Bernard Newdigate called it the best face since the first Caslon, and Stanley Morison said it was "an original face, that is to say, its essential characteristics are not drawn from existing sources, at least as far as the roman is concerned." Those were among the restrained comments. Such enthusiasm can be explained by reference to the types the previous generation of English designers had been making — Morris, Ricketts, Cobden-Sander-

GRQN

son, Walker, and others. Next to them, or next to most of the American faces from the same era, including those by Bertram Grosvenor Goodhue and Morris Benton, Kennerley is more open, more classical, less mannered; it almost dances. In fact, it dances too much, but that is only in hindsight.

Also evident is a definite fin de siècle tone. The individual letters do not easily reveal its source, but it is there. Aubrey Beardsley lurks around this type at least as much as the Renaissance type designers do.

Goudy says he based Kennerley on the canon size of Fell types illustrated in Horace Hart's *Notes on a Century of Typography at the University Press, Oxford.*[16] That volume, produced in only one hundred and fifty copies, is not often seen now, but the Fell types can be found in many of the standard books on typefaces. They were designed in France in the seventeenth century and bought by an agent of Bishop John Fell of Oxford from Abraham van Dyck, the son of the great type cutter Christoffel van Dyke, in the Netherlands.

Fell is a darker face than Kennerley; it sinks into the page and draws the eye down into it. Kennerley has more rounded and open characters, and, while the contrast between thick and thin lines is much less pronounced than in Fell,

some of the thinner stems and hairlines are so attenuated that they look decorative. Updike's judgment that the roman lower case tends to roll and the italic is too uniform is right.

Henry Lewis Bullen said later that when Goudy was designing this face he worked from a copy of Nicolas Jenson's 1470 Eusebius. That is an interesting suggestion. Goudy was devouring old books

Above: Capital letters in Kennerley Old Style
Below: Showings of Kennerley types, from Typographica *No. 5*
Opposite, below: Passage set in Kennerley Old Style, from Typographica *No. 5*

at the time and picked up hints from many sources. Kennerley clearly owes more to the earliest types than it does to Fell, but trying to trace it to any one of them is fruitless, and Bullen's remark that it was "spoilt Jenson" is ridiculous.

The roman had many imitators, but some characteristics make it still easily identifiable — the relatively high ascenders and short

IT IS OUR DUTY TO COR-rect the errors of books and to
Kennerley Old Style

THIS IS THE APOLOGY of John Froben for his typo-
Kennerley Bold

ℂ PLATO BOUGHT SOME books by Philolalus for 100 minæ.
Kennerley Old Style Italic

RECTORS OF THE HIGH est ability, among them Jno.
Kennerley Bold Italic

MWEF

descenders, the spur on the G, the odd tails of R and Q, the bold broad stroke on the very wide N. In fact, some of those characteristics make useful a comparison of Kennerley not with Fell or Jenson but with the seventeenth-century face inaccurately called Janson by modern foundries, especially in the upper case roman letters. In the Janson face, the distinctive shape of M, the sweep of the cross

bar in N, the W in which the upstroke of the left V meets the downstroke of the right one at midpoint, the position of the tail on Q, and shapes of E and F — all have telling echoes in Kennerley. Herman Zapf redesigned some sizes of Jenson for the Stempel Foundry, referring to the original matrices, which Stempel owns, and one can spend some amusing hours comparing his Janson with Kennerley.

Kennerley italic, made seven years after the roman, is upright and has marked pen qualities. The models for it were fifteenth-century faces, but Goudy rejected the Italian rounding of such lower case letters as b and h. His mixing of principles results in a stiffening of the letters in lines of type.

Goudy Old Style

This face was designed for Ameri-

can Type Founders in 1915. The capitals are based on lettering in a Renaissance painting. For decades Goudy said it was by Holbein, but in 1944 he admitted he had never been able to find the painting again and could not prove it was a Holbein. It hardly matters. Renaissance painters looked to architectural models for lettering in their pictures, and that would have appealed to Goudy. When the type first appeared Henry Lewis Bullen was ecstatic about it, and Updike thought the capitals had "an agreeable freedom, and they compose into strong lines of dignified letter."

The lower case — Goudy had hoped it would be "in perfect harmony with classic capitals which harked back to a period some hundreds of years earlier" — owes most to Nicolas Jenson, but many other influences are evident, including Bodoni. Goudy complained that "the short descenders which I allowed American Type Founders to inveigle me into giving p, q, g, j, and y — though only under protest" marred the face.

The type is not entirely old style as that term was understood in Goudy's time. The overall impression is of faces made before the late seventeenth century, but there are many variations. The capitals and lower case work well together. The capitals have small serifs that gain visible strength

THIS FACE was designed in 1911 for use in a sumptuous presentation of ten short stories by H. G. WELLS published by MITCHELL KENNERLEY & was afterward offered to printers generally. A modest showing in *Typographica No. 1* of the two sizes then available brought response at once from printers, and the demand, in spite of its piration by certain unscrupulous machine men, today is as great as ever. It is an original face; that is to say, its essential characteristics are not drawn from existing sources. One writer says "Kennerley besides being beautiful in detail, is beautiful in mass; and the letters set into words seem to lock into one another which is common in the letter of early printers, but is rare in modern type."

Frederic W. Goudy

Goudy Old Style roman

Frederic W. Goudy

Kennerley roman

Frederic W. Goudy

Goudy Old Style italic

Frederic W. Goudy

Kennerley italic

Opposite: Page from "The Goudy
Family," booklet published by
American Type Founders and set
in Goudy Old Style

from bracketing and further sturdiness from the fact that vertical strokes look brush made, not quite straight, as though they were searching for surer footing. The lower case is more rounded than one would find in Renaissance models, and together upper and lower case in sentences give the impression that the lower case letters are anchored to the capitals and are trying to pull away; there is a tautness in lines of this type that escaped Goudy in his earlier designs.

If one is curious about how much Goudy learned in a few years, a comparison of the Goudy Old Style roman with Kennerley will be enlightening. They are brothers, but the younger one has all the advantages.

Goudy Old Style italic, made long before Kennerley italic, is much closer to sixteenth-century models than the Kennerley, but, even though the letters are narrower than the roman letters of Old Style, they, like those of the Kennerley italic, reveal Goudy's tendency to round characters. Goudy claimed it is "an original letter… I believe the first distinctive italic in modern times." Perhaps. It was different from any available for some generations and was widely used and copied. It is certainly one of the finest italics Goudy made.

American Type Founders made a celebration of the design of Goudy Old Style. Morris Benton of A.T.F. made bold versions of it that A.T.F. promoted, along with Goudy's designs, very successfully. Goudy's account is significant:

From the parent design the American Type Founders Company developed Goudy Bold, Extra Bold, and Italics, to form a combination called the "Goudy Family" but with which I had abso-

THIS admirable type design shows a strong affinity with the classic roman types of the early Italian printers, yet enlivened by more contrast of main and minor lines as well as by more acute serifs. It is an early Venetian roman design, modernized for present-day purposes, with a quality of its own which may perhaps best be expressed by the word "flowing." While the Goudy design is classically correct, the appearance of restraint and stiffness is missing. All its refinements make for the prime requisite of clarity or readability. The light shines freely through each character to define the lines of which it is composed. The Goudy family invites analysis. It may please you at a glance. We think it will; but, like all those who are proud of their products, we prefer the purchaser who buys with appreciative understanding rather than the one who buys simply upon the impulse of admiration

Cloister Initial

1

lutely no part; nor did I ever receive any compensation for this use of my name. Also, by enlarging the small capitals to a height almost that of the type body — thereby increasing the weight of the letters — a new character was developed which was named "Goudy Title." To permit a larger face without kern, the "Q" was redesigned at the foundry to a form which irritates me mightily.

Goudy Modern

Goudy Modern, designed in 1918, has remained remarkably popular for seven decades. Joseph Blumenthal, who surveyed the first fifty years of the Best Books of the Year awards voted on by members of the American Institute of Graphic Arts, noted that it was used more than any other face.

To see it as it was used by two

very great printers, one ought to look at Sir Francis Meynell's Nonesuch edition of the complete works of Shakespeare (Meynell obviously thought very highly of it; he used it in two other Nonesuch books) and at William Everson's "Granite and Cypress." Goudy himself displayed it majestically in *Ars Typographica* No. 2, and it is a good idea to study that journal for a notion of what he thought this face could do. But the Nonesuch Shakespeare and "Granite and Cypress" are the definitive appearances of Goudy Modern. The Everson volume is one of the great pieces of printing done in any century, and a reader who wants education about the look of words on a page should get to a rare book collection and see it. Everson's pages are a rebuke to anyone who does not especially

like the letters of this font; in them these characters are like ragamuffins become Roman senators, as warm as they are stately.

For a type with such deep color, the Modern does have the open look Stanley Morison praised it for in the *Fleuron*. He found it "strikingly handsome in the mass" and said that "in spite of the fact that it is, on the whole, a condensed fount, the weight is so nicely judged and the thicks and thins so cleverly adjusted that the effect is rather generous and open."

Strictly speaking, the designation "modern" is inaccurate. As Goudy acknowledged, it has features of old style faces. There are some instructive comparisons that can be made. Goudy Modern roman should be looked at next to some other popular faces of the era, such as Vale and Morris's Golden. Next to the nobly erect Goudy Modern the Vale type appears so romanesque it seems to crouch; the side-by-side comparison will reveal a lot about how that effect is achieved. Goudy Modern looks like Golden sprung free. What it sprang free from is a kind of architectural rigidity that many good turn-of-the-century types had. In fact, one can have some fun putting a page of Goudy Modern next to one in Bertram Grosvenor Goodhue's Merrymount type, a very architectural type made for Updike's press; the Goodhue type is so thick and upright it suggests pillars as much as letters. One other exercise I have found useful in quieting some of my own prejudices against this face is to compare pages of it with some of Robert Estienne's celebrated sixteenth-century ones. Goudy's roman letters in this type look as open and classical as most of those Estienne used, yet the face has a very modern look in comparison.

GRANITE & CYPRESS · ROBINSON JEFFERS · RUBBINGS FROM THE ROCK POEMS GATHERED FROM HIS STONEMASON YEARS WHEN SUBMISSION TO THE SPIRIT OF GRANITE IN THE BUILDING OF HOUSE & TOWER & WALL FOCUSED HIS IMAGINATION & GAVE MASSIVE PERMANENCE TO HIS VERSE THE LIME KILN PRESS · THE UNIVERSITY OF CALIFORNIA AT SANTA CRUZ ANNO DOMINI MCMLXXV

Above: Title-page of William Everson's 1975 edition of "Granite and Cypress" set in Goudy Modern
Opposite: Settings of Goudy Modern roman and italic, from Typographica *No. 5*

IN GOUDY Modern Mr. Goudy has taken for his model a letter used by the French engravers of the 18th century for the captions to their engravings. He

Goudy Modern

THE SPIRIT of Goudy Modern Italic is in the direction of freedom, but with consistency. It has a decided quality of elegance that is entirely its own. It has no prototype.

Goudy Modern Italic

It should definitely be compared with two of Goudy's other types — Klaxon and Goethe. Klaxon was an advertising face done a few years earlier for the maker of the car horns, and it is clearly a forerunner. Goudy Modern is related even more closely to the much later Goethe type, which it inspired. In Goethe, Goudy made the kinds of changes one suspects he would have made in Goudy Modern if it had not become so popular that he did not dare redraw it. The Goethe face is much more beautiful. If Goudy had worked on it more, it might have become the outstanding type in his entire canon. But, unfortunately, he designed it at the invitation of the committee in Dresden that was planning the Goethe bicentennial, and shortly after it was submitted Germany was transformed into Hitler's Third Reich. Once that change happened, there was little interest in Germany in getting a type from Goudy, and Goudy had little incentive to go

on working on the Goethe. I think anyone who looks at pages of it — it was used in the Limited Editions Club's *Frankenstein* — next to pages of Goudy Modern will not only see an interesting family history but will wish Goudy had worked more on the Goethe. His intention, he said, was to make Goethe darker than it is. Many people think its superiority to its ancestor derives in part from its lightness, but I am not sure that a deeper color would not improve it.

The italic of Goudy Modern fits very well with the roman, but owes only a little to it, and is remarkably original altogether. To my eye the lower case letters on the whole are wider than an italic ought to be, but this type looks very good on a page.

Oddly enough, Goudy Modern is really an afterthought. It is actually Goudy Open with the white spaces filled in. About that face, Goudy's account suggests another comparison to be made with Goudy

Modern. Goudy Open was inspired, he says, by the caption of a French engraving used as the frontispiece for Alfred Pollard's *Fine Books*. That eighteenth-century engraving depicts a scene from Ovid. The caption does not have all the letters of the alphabet in it, so Goudy obviously took from it inspiration for a look in a typeface, not models for all the letters (in fact, the lettering of the caption is very different from Goudy Modern in most respects). In any case, Goudy said of the caption:

The letter forms had something of a "modern" look; but in an attempt to give a quality of interest and legibility which the "modern" types of Bodoni lacked, I bravely increased (unlike Bodoni and his school) the weight of the hairlines, bracketed the serifs slightly, and carried my curves more generously toward the stems. In this way I gave strength to the letters constructively and avoided the appearance in print of a "mere jumble of heavy lines fretted here

and there with greyness," a quality in Bodoni's types which requires constant adjustment of the eye and focus and constitutes the essential fault of his letter.

Goudy was strangely reticent about Goudy Modern, but he did like Goudy Open a lot.

Garamont

Perhaps too much has been written about this type ever since it first appeared. Stanley Morison, who had persuaded the English Monotype Company to produce its own version of Claude Garamond's type and disliked Goudy's terribly, wrote Updike that he assumed Goudy had simply reproduced the letters found at the end of F. A. Duprat's *Histoire de l'Imprimerie Imperiale de France*. In fact, they came from the four-volume edition of Claudin's *Histoire de l'Imprimerie en France au XV et XVI Siècle*, so Morison's guess was close enough.

Goudy's supporters at the time caused considerable irritation in

Monotype Garamont #248

SPQR

When a type design is good, it is not because each individual letter of the alphabet is perfect in form but because there is a feeling of unbroken harmony and rhythm that runs through the whole design, each letter to every other and to all.

Monotype Garamond #648

SPQR

When a type design is good, it is not because each individual letter of the alphabet is perfect in form but because there is a feeling of unbroken harmony and rhythm that runs through the whole design, each letter to every other and to all.

Intertype Garamond

SPQR

When a type design is good, it is not because **each** individual letter of the alphabet is perfect in **form** but because there is a feeling of unbroken **harmony** and rhythm that runs through the whole design, each letter to every other and to all.

Ludlow Garamond

SPQR

When a type design is good, it is not because each individual letter of the alphabet is perfect in form but because there is a feeling of unbroken harmony and rhythm that runs through the whole design, each letter to every other and to all.

Linotype Garamond #3

SPQR

When a type design is good, it is not because each individual letter of the alphabet is perfect in form but because there is a feeling of unbroken harmony and rhythm that runs through the whole design, each letter to every other and to all.

GARAMONT, DRAWN by FREDERIC W. GOUDY for the Lanston Monotype Machine Co., is adapted from types cut by CLAUDE GARAMOND circa 1540, which are the originals of the "old face" school. His capitals are less square and the serifs are more bracketed than the earlier Venetian types. GARAMOND is said to be the first to supply inclined capitals

Above: Passage announcing Garamont, from Typographica *No. 5 Opposite: Settings of five letter- press versions of Garamond. Goudy designed the Monotype Garamont*

the world of printers by writing extravagant appraisals of the face, which, they claimed, showed all kinds of interesting Goudyesque variations on the Garamond. One of the people this outpouring irritated was Goudy:

Its final form as drawn by me was not the result of inspiration or genius on my part, but was merely the result of an attempt to reproduce as nearly as possible the form and spirit of the "Garamond" letter. I made no attempt to eliminate the mannerisms or deficiencies of his famous type, realizing that they came not by intention, but rather through the punch-cutter's handling, to his lack of tools of precision and his crude materials....

In fact, Goudy had many fights with the shop workers at the Lanston Company, who kept trying to correct the Garamont oddities when they were cutting matrices.

He was certainly justified in calling it a copy, about as exact as freehand drawing could achieve. The similarity of the roman characters is so striking that one has to admire the accuracy of Goudy's eye. And the italic, except for slight variations in such letters as l, i, and f, is an admirably correct rendering of the face displayed in Garamond's *Caractères de l'Université.*

The long popularity of this face is something of a mystery. The version made by English Monotype at Morison's suggestion is a superior type on the page. It corrects inconsistencies of the Garamond in a way that allows it to be composed in much more readable pages than Goudy's version.

The name Goudy gave this face, with the terminal t instead of d, was the Latin form of the name without a case ending, the form used in books in which Garamond

was listed as publisher.

Goudy Newstyle
Goudy was attached to this type, and it explains much of what he was trying to achieve in his modern faces. If it rewards study, the reward is primarily in the problems it presents. It is very difficult to work with, but some remarkable books have been set in it. It is close fitting, but in this case not even that characteristic quite satisfies Goudy's requirement for readability. Some of the letters do not lose their eccentric character when they are set in words and lines. The q does not fit well with other letters in either the upper or lower case; the lower case g has hairlines that make it tend to disappear among other letters; the roman lower case w has a peculiarly Roman inscription form that is out of place in such a face; and the lower case k remains incongruous no matter how it is placed among its fellow letters.

At its first issue in 1921, Goudy provided more than twenty alternative forms of various letters for the roman font. He wrote several accounts of the origins of these characters, appealing to the notion, fairly common in the early part of the century, that either spelling or writing should be reformed to make clear to everyone how words that look or sound the same in English might be accurately pronounced by a reader unfamiliar with English orthography. Somehow, either the shape of letters or the spellings of words would make clear to a reader the proper sound of the word or its proper meaning.

Goudy adopted a system suggested by the English academic poet Robert Bridges. Bridges suggested using letters of different shapes to indicate different pro-

THE commerce of books comforts me in my age and solitude: it eases me of a troublesome weight of idleness, & delivers me at all hours from company that I dislike; and it blunts the point of griefs, if they are not extreme, and have not got an entire possession of the soul. To divert myself from a troublesome fancy, 'tis to run to my Books; they presently fix me to them, and drive the other out of my thoughts; and do not mutiny to see that I have only recourse to them for want of other more real, natural, and lively conveniences; they always receive me with the same kindness. I never travel without Books, either in peace or

Left: Passage set in Goudy Newstyle, from Typographica *No. 5*
Opposite: Page from "Italian Old Style," booklet designed by Bruce Rogers and published by the Lanston Monotype Machine Company, 1924

nunciations. Thus Goudy had different letter forms to indicate how to pronounce g as in gee and g as in against. The method went on and on. Even printers who were initially taken with the type did not use these odd characters, and eventually, when Goudy recut the entire font and made some changes, he dropped all the alternative characters.

Newstyle does have the testimony of some great printers and typographers in its favor. The Grabhorns had set a hundred pages of their edition of Whitman's *Leaves of Grass* in Lutetia when they first saw Newstyle; they destroyed the work they had done and reset the entire book in this face. It is a magnificent book and a great tribute to the skill of the Grabhorns.

Goudy's fondness for the type was shared by Bruce Rogers. In fact, when the Oxford University Press asked Rogers to design the famous Lectern Bible, he originally intended to use Goudy New-style for it, even though he thought even then that there were problems with a few of the letters. Eventually Oxford persuaded him to set the Lectern Bible in his own Centaur type. When Goudy was eighty, however, he and Rogers conferred about Newstyle and agreed on modifications that Rogers wanted to make. Several years later Lanston Monotype issued the face still called Goudy Bible, which is a slightly redesigned version of Goudy Newstyle, done by Rogers and Sol Hess of the Lanston company for Rogers's World Bible. In general Rogers and Hess made some letters narrower and modified half a dozen lower case characters and as many capitals. These changes were enough to give Rogers the compact look that he wanted and to tone down the appearance of Newstyle somewhat. The result is stunning as it appears in the World Bible, which is a much more satisfying Bible to look at than the Lectern Bible.

Italian Old Style
Knowledgeable people have nearly come to blows over this face. Its admirers and its detractors are many and vociferous. The detractors do not say it is a bad type, merely that it is not as good as others in the same style — say, Bruce Rogers's Centaur — and that it has been vastly overpraised. The admirers have claimed that among other things it is one of the best versions ever made of a Renaissance face for use in modern times. Goudy did spend a lot of his life in that search. Indeed, some critics have said he kept designing the same type over and over in his quest. To my eye it is fine type, one of the best old styles available. It is far from foolproof for a compositor, but it has been used in some very beautiful books. A curious reader should have a look at Goudy's book *A Half-Century of Type Design and Typography* to see how good it can look.

One of its admirers was Rog-

EARLY PRINTERS
IN THE CITY OF
VENICE

From Dibdin's Bibliographical Decameron

THE FOURTH DAY

¶SPEAKERS:
Lysander.
Philemon.
Lisardo.
Almansa.

¶COMMENTS:
John de Spira, parent of the Venetian press.] This point, I submit, is now triumphantly established by the existing privilege of the Senate of Venice, granted to John de Spira, of the date of September the 18th, 1469. A copy of this privilege was transmitted to Denis, by the Abbé Morelli, & appears in the *Suffragium pro Johanne de Spira Primo Venetiarum Typographo, Viennæ,* 1794, 8vo. of the former. It is too important not to occupy some twenty lines in this present note. Le voici!'1469, *Die 18 Septembris.* Inducta est in hanc nostram inclytam civitatem ars imprimendi libros, in diesque magis celebrior et frequentior fiet, per operam studium et ingenium Magistri Ioannis de Spira, qui ceteris aliis urbibus hanc nostram præelegit,

LYSANDER

T IS now really time to notice the rise & early progress of the typographical art in one other great Italian city: and you will perhaps readily give a guess in what other city this may be?

PHILEMON ⎱ Venice!
LISARDO ⎰

LYSANDER

¶Twice accurately spoken! 'The nurse (as Philemon the other day not inaptly expressed it) of ten thousand useful & elegant arts, the central mart of European commerce, the city both of Jenson and of Titian, it was reserved for Venice to give a different turn, and to adopt a purer style, in the productions of its first printers.' All hail to thee, JOHN DE SPIRA, parent of the Venetian press! * I see thee yonder, in

liæ, et artificum mercede, præstanda sit materia, ut alacrius perseveret, artemque suam imprimendi potius celebriorem reddere, quam desinere, habeat; quemadmodum in aliis exercitiis sustentandis, et

ubi cum coniuge liberis et familiâ totâ suâ inhabitaret, exerceretque dictam artem librorum imprimendorum : iamque summâ omnium commendatione impressit *Epistolas Ciceronis,* et nobile opus *Plinii de Naturali Historia* in maximo numero, et pulcherrima litterarum forma, pergitque quotidie alia præclara volumina imprimere; adeo ut industria et virtute huius hominis, multisque praeclarisque voluminibus, et quidem pervili pretio, locupletabitur. Et quoniam tale inventum ætatis nostræ peculiare et proprium, priscis illis omnino incognitum, omni favore et ope augendum atque fovendum est, eidemque Magistro Joanni, qui magno urgetur sumptu familiæ multo quidem inferioribus, fieri solitum est; infrascripti Domini Consiliarii ad humilem et devotam supplicationem prædicti Magistri Joannis terminarunt, terminandoque decreverunt, ut per annos quinque proxime futuros nemo omnino sit, qui velit, possit, valeat, audeatve exercere dictam artem imprimendorum librorum in hac inclyta civitate Venetiarum, et districto suo, nisi ipse Magister Joannes. Et toties, quoties aliquis inventus fuerit, qui contra hanc terminationem et decretum ausus fuerit exercere ipsam artem et imprimere libros; multari condemnarique debeat, et amittere instrumenta et libros impressos. Et sub hâc eadem pœna nemo debeat, aut possit tales libros in aliis terris et locis impressos vendendi causa huc portare,[1]

> Angelus Gradenico.
> Bertuccius Contareno.
> Angelus Venerio.   } *Consiliarii.*'
> Jacobus Mauroceno.
> Franciscus Dandulo.

❡ This document is curious on many accounts. It informs us, if we were not already informed by his own colophons, that I. de Spira printed the *Epistles of Cicero* before the *Pliny*—and, what is rather strange, that he had a *five years patent or privilege for exclusive printing at Venice!* How came it then to pass that Jenson opened his press in 1470, and continued, for many successive years, a popular printer at Venice? Was the privilege granted to I. de Spira only conditionally—if he should so long live?[2] There is no accounting for the rival press of Jenson upon any other ground. As to the date of 1461, in the *Decor Puellarum*, that point is now at rest: it being, beyond all further reasonable doubt, an error for the date of 1471. See the authorities referred to in the *Bibl. Spenceriana*, vol. iv. p. 116-118. Of the *Familiar Epis-*

imagination, pale, emaciated, and breathless: living only just to witness the completion of thy *Cicero* and *Pliny*—to clasp thy barely commenced *St. Austin* to thy breast, and to expire in the embrace! See, he dies in the arms of his brother, VINDELIN; who, on his decease, conducted the business with great credit and success for many subsequent years, and who has proved himself to be worthy of the mantle which his brother cast upon him.

tles of Cicero, the first effort of his press, there are two editions—in the same year —1469; which have been particularly described in the work last referred to, vol. i. p. 321-3. The Blenheim and the McCarthy libraries each contain a copy of one of these impressions UPON VELLUM. The *Pliny*, upon paper, is in Lord Spencer's collection: but how can I convey an adequate idea of its condition and amplitude? Think, enthusiastic collector, of the uncontaminated snow upon the highest of the Apennine peaks, & you will have an idea of the size and colour of the Spencerian copy of the first *Pliny!* The press-work of this surprising volume is quite perfect. I have carefully examined it with that of the earliest and latest specimens of Jenson's press, and it 'beats them all hollow!' Yet remember, Spira-loving reader, that the Imperial library at Vienna contains a copy of this very first Pliny UPON VELLUM! Who, that hath drank deeply and freely at the fountain-head of Bibliomania, would not make a pilgrimage to such a shrine?

❡ Let it however be observed that, generally speaking, the Pliny of 1469 is by no means a very rare book, (see the B. S. vol. ii. p. 253-6,) notwithstanding, from the colophon, only one hundred copies of it appear to have been struck off—and these within the short space of three months![3] The knowing will remember that there are no Greek letters introduced; but that the Greek passages are rendered by means of Roman types.

❡ VINDELIN DE SPIRA, as Lysander above properly intimates, carried on the business which his brother had successfully established. The matchless collection of Lord Spencer contains, I believe, all Vindelin's known works of the date of 1470, with the exception of the *Priscian;* of which,

Below: "Saks Fifth Avenue,"
broadside, 1934
Opposite: Page from "Italian
Old Style"

ers, who said he thought it showed the influence of the roman letter of the Renaissance master Bernhard Ratdolt. That is not an unambiguous remark. Goudy had said he relied on Jenson, and Rogers was saying something about his fidelity to that face. But, as usual, Goudy's borrowings were not literal. Ratdolt's type is illustrated in many of the standard books on the history of type, and anyone interested in a comparison should set it down next to not only Italian Old Style but also Goudy Antique, which was cut five years earlier, in 1919. The similarities between Goudy Antique and Ratdolt are evident on sight.

Italian Old Style has a definite relation to Jenson's type of 1470. But there are differences between it and both Jenson's and Ratdolt's type. Both of the old types have a more upstanding appearance on the page. Italian Old Style looks stouter, partly because its color is deeper and it fits more closely. "The individual letters are quite full and round," Goudy wrote, "and with their close fitting give an impression of luxuriousness combined with legibility, simplicity, and dignity." About that he was right.

Rogers used Italian Old Style along with his Centaur in the Grolier Society's edition of the *Champ Fleury* of Geoffroy Tory to wonderful effect. But the locus classicus for this type is the display sheet Rogers designed for the Lanston Monotype Company when it first issued the type. Based on pages of texts of biblical commentary and other theological treatises of the Renaissance that reflect a manuscript tradition receding into Roman times, with different sizes of letters set in ways to give differing emphases surrounding a central text, it is a great instruction for compositors

Saks Fifth Avenue

THIS is *the first showing* of a new type face designed especially for Saks by Fred W. Goudy. He has not attempted any radical departures from good tradition, but some of the individual characters will be found to present unusual features which contribute to its novel effect in mass, and at the same time add a decorative touch entirely in harmony with their kin without loss of legibility.

These added lines show the design of the italic. This is Mr. Goudy's ninety-second type face and has been named Saks-Goudy.

and printers. How could anyone who owns a copy resist framing and mounting it? At the time it was issued, the display could be had free from Lanston, but there are a number of contemporary accounts of its being sold in bookstores as the prime demonstration of Rogers's art.

The italic face is not so satisfying. Its color is not as uniform, and that variation tends to make pages of it distracting. It is simply too wide to be a good italic, and it makes at best an indifferent companion to the roman. Also, it is open and rolling to the point of annoyance. It is quite close, actually, to italics of some mid-sixteenth-century Florentine printers who, it seems to me, anticipated in their types the whole Baroque style.

Saks Goudy
When Saks Fifth Avenue introduced this face in 1934, it made a

terrific show of the debut, with a party and an exhibit at the National Arts Club and receptions and dinners in several Manhattan hotels, as well as private receptions for Goudy. The store bought pages of advertisements in newspapers and magazines set in Saks Goudy to announce that from then on the type would be the Saks signature.

Goudy loved the hoopla. When the advertising manager of the store visited him at Deepdene and asked what material he was engraving matrices in, he told her it was gold instead of brass. She later sent him a bar of gold of roughly the right size and, after some frustrating trials, Goudy engraved a G in it. Saks then presented the gold matrix to the Vassar College library in a big ceremony.

Critics of Goudy are fond of saying that all his types are advertising faces. That is obviously not true, but he knew how to make a

fine type for advertising, and this is one. It has in it a lot of what he had learned from working for many years on book faces, but it violates all kinds of norms for those types. I think many people who have been very severe about the Saks have forgotten what it was meant for.

In the roman Goudy produced the effect of brilliance by doing pretty much what he was so often annoyed with Bodoni for doing — he made all the stems heavy and all the hairlines light. The roman capitals are by far the best part of this font. They have a suggestion of the classical without being monumental, and in the large sizes they are very graceful and powerful. Overall, the face has deep color without seeming as bold as it really is. If you look closely at the letters you will realize how much ink they lay on a page, but when you glance at the page they seem simply striking, not impressively dark.

Goudy was provokingly hyperbolical in his own appraisal of this type. "I believe that Saks Goudy is as good a type as I have ever made, or can make," he wrote, "and that the italic is one of the best italics I have ever done." I know of no one who would agree with that judgment, and I doubt Goudy ever thought anyone would. The italic in this font is interesting mostly for its indication that Goudy had returned to his earlier fascination with Art Nouveau. It is quite upright. The bowls of a, b, d, and p are very open for an italic face. But it is in the vertical lines of the lower case letters that one sees immediately the Art Nouveau effect. In fact that same bending of vertical lines is found in the roman. When roman and italic turn up on the same page so does a hint of a fin de siècle smile. All

GOUDY MEDIAEVAL

Drawings begun Aug. 1 9, 1 6 pt. finished Sept. 1 5, 1 9 3 0

A NEW TYPE is here presented, which, judged by pragmatic standards, may not meet the approval of those critics who demand in their types the elimination of any atavistic tendency. Quite obviously it cannot be judged fairly by the advertising compositor or the job printer, nor must unassuming legibility be made its first criterion. At one time books were entirely written out by hand, but the qualities that made the writing charming defy completely successful reproduction in types. Goudy Mediæval presents a face that in its lower case borrows the freedom of the pen of the Renaissance. Its capitals however, owe less to the pen-hands since they are more or less composites of monastic ms. & painted Lombardic forms. The designer hopes nevertheless, that his capitals will be found in accord with

---

in all, there is more than a hint in Saks Goudy of his earlier work, even of the work he did as a letterer. It makes a connection between his occupations. This is a case in which what the critics say is true and ought to be taken as tribute.

Mediaeval and Franciscan
Mediaeval was made in 1930 and Franciscan in 1932, and the only reason for taking them up together, or at all, is to remind people of a class of typeface that has fallen out of use. Faces of this kind were important for about fifty years, and it would not be surprising to see them, or some form of them,

HAHBHCHDH
HLHMHNHOF
HVHWHXHYH
OCODOEOEC
ÒMÒNÒQỌ̀̇̇̇

Top: "Goudy Mediaeval," broadside, 1930
Above: Setting of Franciscan, 1932
Opposite: Page from "Good King Wenceslas," showing first use of Franciscan, 1932

come back. The class, in Goudy's case, includes those he called text types. Such faces were popular for a long time with printers and designers, who thought they gave a medieval, or black letter, appearance to a page. In part, that desire was a hangover from the long love of Gothic architecture in Europe and this country. For reasons not justified by historical scholarship, that architectural taste was associated with a dark, black letter, or fraktur, look in type.

Goudy described Mediaeval as "one of my most original designs." He claimed it was based on a twelfth-century German manuscript hand.

To me it looks factitious, and Goudy said as much when he wrote that "in its lower case, [it] borrows the freedom of the scribe's pen of the Renaissance; its capitals...are more or less composites of monastic manuscript and Lombardic painted forms."

Franciscan is the name given by Edwin Grabhorn to the redesigned and recut Aries face Goudy did in 1926 for Spencer Kellogg's Aries Press. That face was based on the Subiaco type designed by Emery Walker and S. C. Cockerell for St. John Hornby's Ashendene Press. Grabhorn used the Franciscan for his edition of *The Spanish Occupation of California*, a book that won the highest honors in the Fifty Best Books of the Year competition conducted by the American Institute of Graphic Arts in 1934.

The Franciscan, as well as the Aries, is much more open than Subiaco and much more angular. It is closer to a true black face, in the bold perhaps even a true fraktur, but without the shattered and torn look of most frakturs.

Some attention to the black face types will reward a student. They teach one some essential qualities of handwriting and the shapes of letters that roman faces do not, qualities that are important for designers to appreciate. For anyone with a sense of humor about the motions of the hand holding a pen, Goudy's later Tory Text makes a good comparison with Mediaeval and Franciscan. He said he "enjoyed every minute of its making," and I believe him, but I wouldn't want to have to set it or design a page using it. It was inspired by the *lettres batârde* in the Grolier edition of Tory's *Champ Fleury*. And that is a book that anyone with a sense of humor about anything ought to see.

GOOD
KING WENCESLAS

A Carol by
Dr. John Mason Neale

☙

I

GOOD King Wences-
las look'd out
On the feast of
Stephen,
When the snow lay round about,
Deep, and crisp, and even.
Brightly shone the moon that night,
Though the frost was cruel,
When a poor man came in sight
Gath'ring winter fuel.

I wonder how many designers or printers now could turn a fine compliment from another art and hope to be understood by others in his profession. At the ceremony sponsored by the American Institute of Graphic Arts in 1921 for the presentation of its gold medal to Goudy, George W. Jones said "Fred Goudy never did any harm to typography." That elegant compliment comes from the Hippocratic oath. The principle used to be drummed into doctors not in the Greek of its author but in Latin, still the common language of science at the turn of the century. *Primum non nocere* — the first thing is not to do any harm — was painted on the walls of medical schools and even in operating rooms. There was a barb in Jones's compliment, but of a kind Goudy liked; it tickled more than it hurt. It is the tribute of a traditionalist, and at that time it would still have had great force.

What Goudy had fought for for many years in his writing and lecturing was precisely the preservation of the long tradition of type design and type making. But because he tried to extract the heart of the crafts from traditional methods and make people rethink the tradition in terms of its results, he had made not a few enemies on all sides. Jones was really trying to point out that Goudy was taking the only sensible stand: He wanted designers and printers to use the new technologies but not to lose the esthetic standards that informed the work of the earliest type designers, printers, and publishers.

RETRO-SPECTIVE: WAS HE OR WASN'T HE?

Rightly, Goudy is remembered as a type designer. But in surveying his work, it is necessary to recognize some other significant accomplishments. He used his considerable celebrity to stimulate debate about design and craftsmanship more effectively than anyone else in his age. He was not as learned as some of his contemporaries and not as original in argument, but his writing and lecturing were by no means uninformed or unsophisticated. His repeated suggestion that the old masters were people he or anyone else now might sit down and talk with is a very canny argument to American audiences. He was encouraging designers and printers to think of good design as something essentially modern, even as

Goudy, drawn by Alexander Stern, 1938

Alexander Stern '38

FWGoudy

*Below: Goudy, scratchboard
portrait by Charles E. Pont
Opposite: Goudy, linoleum-
block print by Frank Heger*

it was in the fifteenth century, and not as a privileged or learned art.

His defense of new technologies and his unfailing curiosity about them were part of his overall argument, and his insistence that the great designers of the past would have used those technologies if they had had them was an encouragement not to throw over old traditions but to make the best of them. In fact, one aspect of Goudy's own method in designing seems peculiarly important now, as computer technology approaches making every designer of a page his own type designer — the freehand drawing of letters. The entire history of letters springs from the hand, and Goudy's reminders that our perception of them as beautiful and useful, even as understandable, springs from our knowledge of them as having begun with writing and drawing is wise. Drawing letters that are to become types is fundamental to understanding their human dimensions and their place in the history of human expression, and it is precisely when technology becomes most advanced that an individual's mastery of the underlying craft is crucial to preserving the art.

That raises the further question of how much the modern designer has to know about type and printing, and I think it is clear from Goudy's dedication to tradition what his answer would be. He was a printer before he designed types, and he came to master every step not only in making types but in printing. He would have been suspicious of someone who would try to design a type who did not know the traditional methods of printing, who did not know the effect and quality of a type that makes an impression on

a page as distinguished from off-set, probably even of someone who did not know how a chisel affects the shapes of letters in stone. But behind all those things is the movement of the hand making letters. That is fundamental. And it seems to me that Goudy's refusal to use compasses and rulers, and to reduce pleasing shapes to geometric or mathematical formulas, is an important example now. Beauty springs from the whole imagining human being or it remains unsprung.

Goudy never took his teaching role casually, despite all his efforts to entertain. And in any review of his work one has to give him great credit for *Ars Typographica.* Some of his other publications, notably his books, remain impressive contributions to the literature of design. But in that journal he created an instrument of history and criticism for American designers that was a vital inspiration. It is no discredit to him that it became something quite different in other hands once he left off being editor; even he could not do everything. The numbers he edited made his point, and they have had a lasting influence on the way others have approached design.

Goudy's printing and typography, his design of pages and magazines and books, would never have earned him a place in the history of design or printing, but even in those areas, as Jones said, he never did any harm to typography. But, in the end, his reputation rests squarely on his work as a type designer.

Was Goudy the greatest American type designer or the most prolific? I am not sure the questions are very useful, although everyone asks them. His most serious fault as a designer was his eager-

ness to produce too many faces. Even some of his friends noted with annoyance his fascination in the 1930s with reaching the number one hundred in his list of designs, and it is obvious that haste cost him something by way of perfection. A couple of faces he redesigned after some years were vastly improved, and it seems evident that if he had been willing to wait longer before he turned his initial ideas into types he would have made more good faces than he did. It is true that he had to make a living, but by the mid-20s he was doing that fairly well, and necessity cannot excuse all his excesses.

But a dispassionate examination of his designs will yield a number that will stand comparison with the best work of other designers in any era. Goudy Old Style and the accompanying italic are still justly popular among designers, and it is hard to imagine they will not remain so in the future. By now Goudy Modern and italic must be ranked among the classics. One might approach

composition of this type with some hesitation, but its brilliant use by some great compositors and designers proves its distinction beyond any criticism. Something of the same judgment has to be made about Goudy Newstyle. One can argue about whether the changes made in the face by Rogers and Hess improved or disfigured it — and you can get good debaters on both sides of that question — but their changes were not all that extensive and at least some of them were suggested by Goudy. It is certainly his design in either form.

Italian Old Style and its italic have also passed into the list of classics, if the preferences of designers are any measure. It is still used in England and on the Continent as well as in this country, and so often with striking effect that what critics think of as peculiarities in some letters are no great disadvantages. While Deepdene is not as widely used now as Italian Old Style, it is more highly regarded by some very tough critics and designers, and I think it can stand comparison with the

best of the Renaissance designs.

Among Goudy designs that one sees used often, and which have been eloquently appreciated by designers, Goudy Heavy and Goudy Text are two whose charms remain mysterious to me. Goudy himself had serious reservations about both, but then he also had very high opinions of some of his faces that are clearly inferior. On the other hand, far too little is said now about the Venezia italic he made to accompany George Jones's roman. It is surely one of the best italics available and is in fact very widely used in England. In any fair accounting, that design deserves distinction. Forum Title is another face much more extensively used in England now than here, a fact that does honor to English designers who have had the good sense to continue to respect Sir Francis Meynell's very high opinion of it.

Finally, some of Goudy's designs that he would have worked on again if he had had the opportunity are so good one has to regret that he did not — notably Goethe and Marlborough. A man who could produce those designs as quickly as he did, designs that would make anyone wish for more, needs few defenders.

So, he did too much too quickly. But he made somewhere between a dozen and half that number of faces that are among the best types available. That is a great achievement. And when one looks over Goudy's entire work, taking into account both the sheer volume of it and the presence in that work of such a large number of excellent designs, it seems merely silly to deny that he was the outstanding American designer of typefaces and one who has to be considered along with the leading type makers in history.

pack my

box with

lqr jugs r

five dzn z

fl ffi ffi f f ffl ;

- ! ? & ct

Not all the confusion about the listing of Goudy's types is his fault. A list was made for people who attended the 1938 celebration of the thirty-fifth anniversary of the Village Press. Goudy had some part in the preparation of it but did not supervise it, and the record was filled with errors, which he corrected by hand on his own copy. He and Earl Emmons prepared a list that was less inaccurate but not entirely valid or complete. Finally, Goudy wrote *A Half-Century of Type Design and Typography 1895–1945*, published by the Typophiles, to give a complete listing interwoven with a good deal of biography. Its two little volumes are a great pleasure to look at, and many of Goudy's remarks are vastly entertaining. But the book was published in a very limited edition and is not easily found now, so, in the list that follows, I have included a few lengthy comments from it and many shorter ones. In general, all the remarks on the types are taken from it, and those that aren't will be obvious to the reader. I have rejected out of hand any of Goudy's comments that were intended either to straighten out confusions from previous lists or relate this final version to them. I am sure

Goudy drawings for Klaxon, 1914

Goudy's understanding of some of these remarks was clear, but they can be so confusing to anyone else that a few of them might have come from a James Thurber story.

Some of the uncertainty about identification of the Goudy designs arises from the destruction of most of his drawings, matrices, and types in the fire at his shop in 1939. He had some logs and records to work from, along with a great many records of type foundries and from journals and magazines and his own Village Press books. But for many details he had to rely on memory. His recall was celebrated by associates, but one relies on anybody's memory of more than fifty years only with caution.

Another source of confusion, at least until a few years after Goudy's death, were the wild claims made in many articles about him in magazines and newspapers about how many designs he had made. Some people said he had made more than one hundred and thirty faces. At the time of his death, it was common for people to cite 123, even though there are clearly, at best, 122 in *A Half-Century of Type Design*. By now it is to be hoped that the memory of the guesswork done up until forty years ago has disappeared.

Goudy was not careless in his own claims about how many complete typefaces he had made, but he took little effort to correct some of the more extravagant remarks of his admirers. An inspection of the following list will reveal that a number of these designs were not complete faces and that at least one was a mere combination of two other Goudy faces. In his volume on American printers Joseph Blumenthal seems to fault Goudy for counting italic faces as separate ones, even though a large number of them were wholly independent of the roman faces they accompanied. In any case, it seems fair enough to count an italic as a separate face. If one does, it is clear that Goudy designed about one hundred faces altogether.

In my list, the names given the designs are those used by Goudy in *A Half-Century of Type Design*. They do not always correspond exactly to all the different names given through the years in specimen books, magazine articles, and other places, but there is no reason to dispute his designations. To make it more convenient for quick reference, the list is given alphabetically rather than chronologically. For those designs not cast in type, a bracketed notation [nc] follows the name. If there is some doubt, a question mark is included. Where exact dates of completion of the designs are in doubt, the dates are followed by question marks.

Advertisers' Modern, 1930
Goudy could not recall why he started this design or even if all the drawings were finished, but because he had cut all the master patterns he concluded he had done all the other work. It was made for Manuel Rosenberg of Chicago, the publisher of *The Advertiser*, for his annual *Sketch Book*.

The Advertiser's
SKETCH BOOK
1937

Advertisers' Roman [nc], 1917
Patterns were never cut and the drawings were lost in the 1939 fire. Goudy felt it was just as well they perished, "for I don't think they were any too good."

Aries, 1926
Made for Spencer Kellogg's Aries Press in Eden, New York, and begun in 1925, this face was based on the Subiaco type used by St. John Hornby at the Ashendene Press. It has a very Gothic look and was the parent of the much more successful Franciscan face done years later for Edwin Grabhorn. The Aries Press printed at least one book in this type, and there may be more.

T SCOWRETH all scurfe and scalds from the head, being therewith dailie washt before meales. Being moderatlie taken [saith he] it sloweth age, it strengtheth youth, it helpeth digestion, it cutteth flegme, it lighteneth the mind, it quickeneth the spirits, it cureth the hydropsie, it healeth the Strangurie, it pounceth the stone, it expelleth gravel, it puffeth awayes all ventositie, it keepeth and preserveth the head from whirling, the eies from dazeling, the toong from lisping, the mouth from maffling, the teeth from chattering, and the throte from ratling; it keepeth the weasan from stifling, the stomach from wambling,

Atlantis [nc], 1935

In *A Half-Century of Type Design* Goudy said that of designs numbered 87, 88, 95, 96, 98, 99, 102, 103, and 104 in *The Record of Goudy Types* assembled by him and Earl Emmons "absolutely nothing remains after the fire either in proof or in my recollection." He added that "the designs as we named them were: Goudy Book, Hudson, Textbook Old Style, Hasbrouck, Atlantis, Millvale, Mercury, and sketches for two unnamed." In a footnote he said: "These names sound as though copied from Pullman sleepers!"

Booklet Old Style, 1916

This face was named for Goudy's first press and was designed for American Type Founders. Since A.T.F. never displayed it in specimen books, presumably they found it unacceptable. That is a pity; for its time it is a good face and might have had a good influence.

One of the that all attempt lasting lesson for graft pers bright see these song notes stone shone those nests co the seventh regiment rollin SHE SEES HOMES SHE

Barron's Boston News Letter, 1904

This face was designed for Joseph Barron's financial newsletter in Boston. American Type Founders had Robert Wiebking in Chicago cut matrices for it. But forty years later Goudy could not recall "just what sort of letter I did" for Barron.

Bulmer [nc], 1939

Goudy told Lanston Monotype he thought he could design a lower case to fit the fine capitals in a copy of *Hobbinal* printed by William Bulmer in 1813, but his effort was a failure.

Bertham, 1936

In May 1936, Laurence Siegfried, editor of *The American Printer*, asked Goudy for an article on his one-hundredth typeface. Goudy said that the ninety-eighth and ninety-ninth were not "done" — his word — at the time, but he set to work on this one, named for his wife (Bertha M.), who had died the year before, and finished it in sixteen days. He based it on a book set in type derived from one used by Leonard Holle to print the *Geographica* of Ptolemy at Ulm in 1482. Since the Ashendene Press had been using a type made by Emery Walker based on the Holle types, it can be assumed Goudy referred to that face.

ABCDEFGHIJKLMNOP
QRSTUVWXYZ& .,';:!?-
abcdefghijklmnopqrstuv
wxyz fi ff fl ct st 1234567890

Speaking of earlier types, Goudy says:
The old fellows stole all of our best ideas.

Camelot, 1896

This is the first type attributed to Goudy based on letters he drew and sent to the Dickinson Type Foundry. He made only the capitals, and the foundry men added a lower case.

ABCDEFGHIJKLMNOPQ
RSTUVWXYZ& .,';:!?-
$1234567890

Caslon Revised [nc], 1905
Clarence Marder asked for a type like William Caslon's Old Style but "without its spottiness." Goudy said his design for Marder "showed some departures from the usual rendering of a traditional typeface, and this may account for its non-appearance as a type."

Collier Old Style, 1919
Even Robert Wiebking, who cut the matrices, thought this type was odd. In 1909 Goudy had seen in the South Kensington Museum in London a page printed by Palme Isingrin in Basle in 1534 that had a peculiar serif on the lower case d. Goudy assumed the serif had been damaged, but he found it interesting and designed an entire face based on it. It was made for Allen Collier of the Procter and Collier advertising agency in Cincinnati, which represented the Procter and Gamble Company. It is a precursor of Goudy Antique, begun in the same year.

ABCDEFGHIJKLMNO
PQRSTUVWXYZabcd
efghijklmnopqrstuvw
xyz&$,;:.-'!?1234567890

Caxton Initials, 1905
The great San Francisco printer John Henry Nash was fond of this set of capitals, but Goudy considered it "a rather clumsy form of Lombardic capitals." American Type Founders issued it for many years.

Companion Old Style, 1927
The 1927 date is Goudy's. The type was actually delivered in March 1928. It was drawn at the request of Henry B. Quinan, art director of *The Woman's Home Companion* magazine. Goudy thought it "one of the most unusual types I have ever made. It incorporates features which deliberately violate tradition as to stress of curve, but which are so handled that attention is not specifically drawn to the innovations introduced." Not many designers now would agree with his notion that it is reticent about its innovations, but it is truly strange.

ABCDEFGHIJ
KLMNOPQRS
TUVWXYZ

ABCDEFGHIJKLMNOP
QRSTUVWXYZ&.,';:!?-
ABCDEFGHIJKLMNOPQRSTUVWXYZ
abcdefghijklmnopqrstuv
wxyzfffifflflffl1234567890

Cloister Initials, 1918
Goudy allowed that this set of capitals was not, strictly speaking, a typeface. American Type Founders had asked for an alphabet in the style of the large, center capital A in *The Alphabet*, and Goudy drew an entire set for them. He said he had not intended it to be cut, but A.T.F. made matrices and sold the type for a while.

Companion Old Style Italic, 1927
The companion to the above roman.

ABCDEFGHIJKLMNOPQRS
TUVWXYZ&abcdefghijklm
nopqrstuvwxyzfiffffiflffl.,';:!?-
ABCDEMPRg&z
Speaking of earlier types, Goudy says:
The old fellows stole all of our best ideas.

Copperplate Gothic, 1905
Goudy's recollection was that this hodgepodge was done for American Type Founders. It was made for Marder, Luse and Company and then taken on by A.T.F. and
can still be found in old A.T.F. specimen books and their old fonts.

ABCDEFGHIJKLMN
OPQRSTUVWXYZ&
$1234567890.,';:!?-
FWG SAYS: THE OLD
FELLOWS STOLE ALL
OF OUR BEST IDEAS.

Deepdene Italic, 1928
See pages 18–26.

ABCDEFGHIJKLMNOPQRS
TUVWXYZ& abcdefghijklm
nopqrstuvwxyz fi ff fff fl ffl ct .,';:!?-
ABCDEGMPRT kzg gg gg gy

Speaking of earlier types, Goudy says:
The old fellows stole all of our best ideas.

Cushing Italic, 1904
Strictly a job, this face. Goudy made it for Clarence Marder to accompany the
Cushing Roman sold by A.T.F. at the time.

ABCDEFGHIJJKLM
NOPQRSTUVWXZ
abcdefghijklmnopqr
stuvwxyz&£$?!-',:;.
1234567890

Deepdene Bold, 1932
See pages 18–26.

ABCDEFGHIJKLMNOP
QRSTUVWXYZ&.,';:!?-
abcdefghijklmnopqrstuvw
xyzfi ff ffi fl ffl$1234567890

Speaking of earlier types,
Goudy says: The old fellows
stole all of our best ideas.

Deepdene, 1927
See pages 18–26.

ABCDEFGHIJKLMNOP
QRSTUVWXYZ&.,';:!?-
ABCDEFGHIJKLMNOPQRSTUVWXYZ&
abcdefghijklmnopqrstuv
wxyzfi ff ffi fl ffl [ ] 1234567890

Speaking of earlier types, Goudy says:
The old fellows stole all of our best ideas.

Deepdene Bold Italic, 1933
See pages 18–26.

ABCDEFGHIJKLMNOP
QRSTUVWXYZ&.,';:!?-
abcdefghijklmnopqrstuvw
xyzfi ff ffi fl ffl$1234567890

Speaking of earlier types,
Goudy says: The old fellows
stole all of our best ideas.

Deepdene Medium, 1931
See pages 18–26.

ABCDEFGHIJKLMNO
PQRSTUVWXYZ&
abcdefghijklmnopqrstuv
wxyzfiflffffifflffl

De Vinne Roman, 1898
A book face based on the display type designed by Theodore De Vinne and made on the order of Walter Marder of the Central Type Foundry of St. Louis, Missouri.

THE TIMES WHEN ADVERTISERS INSISTED UPON A HEAVY BLACKFACE OR Gothic in displaying advertisements are past. The educational forces that are at work in printing have wrought so well that there is widespread appreciation in evidence of the beauty and value of the refined and $1234567890 neat light faces

Deepdene Open Text, 1931
See pages 18–26. This face was made specifically for *Fashions in American Typography*, published by Goudy's friend Edmund Gress.

This proof shows a new open text in 24 point now in process of cutting It is suited for printing where a touch less austere is wanted than simpler type would allow These characters are set in a face of similar design for use if more color is desired

Display Roman [nc?], 1897
An early experiment, which Goudy described only as "a display letter leaning to the bold."

Deepdene Text, 1931
See pages 18–26. This is simply filled-in Deepdene Open Text.

In the best books men talk to to us their most precious tho pour their souls into ours. Th for books! They are the wor

Engravers' Roman [nc?], 1904
Goudy was uncertain whether this type was ever cut. There is no record of it. It was intended for the use of printers in small towns who had no access to copperplate engravers. Goudy was uppity about it: "Today [1944], I would refuse even to consider such a commission."

Forum Title, 1911
This elegant capital face was based on inscriptions Goudy had made rubbings from on Trajan's Column and the Arch of Titus in Rome in 1910. It was a favorite of Sir Francis Meynell and Bruce Rogers, among others.

ABCDEFGHIJKLMN
OPQRSTUVWXYZ&
1234567890´.,

FWG SAYS · THE OLD FELLOWS
STOLE ALL OF OUR BEST IDEAS

Garamont, 1921
See pages 103–5.

ABCDEFGHIJKLMNOP
QRSTUVWXYZ&ÆŒ
ABCDEFGHIJKLMNOPQRSTU
VWXYZ&ÆŒfifffffifflfflæœctst
abcdefghijklmnopqrstuv
wxyz.,'';:!?-[($1234567890
Speaking of earlier types,

Franciscan, 1932
Goudy had recut — on his own machinery and by his own hand — the Aries face first made in 1926, intending to "use it for my own printing rather than to offer it for general sale," but he was persuaded to sell it to Edwin Grabhorn, who suggested the new name. See page 96.

ABCDEGFGHIJKLMN
OODQRSTUVWXYZ∾
&&.:;/?!'1234567890
abcdefghijklmnopqrstuv
wxyzfffiflffifflct
Speaking of earlier types, Goudy says:
The old fellows stole all of our best ideas.

Garamont Italic, 1921
See pages 103–5.

ABCDEFGHIJKLMNO
PQRSTUVWXYZ&ÆŒ
abcdefghijklmnopqrstuvwxyz
æœfifffffifflffl.,';:!?-$1234567890

Speaking of earlier types,
Goudy says: The old fellows
stole all of our best ideas.

Friar, 1937
Goudy's comment was that he designed this type for his own amusement. He said he based the capitals on the "square capitals" of the fourth century and the "rustic hands" of medieval scribes. The lower case derived from uncials of the fourth, fifth, sixth, and eighth centuries and from types designed by Victor Hammer and Rudolf Koch.

 AABCDEEFGHNIJKLMNO
PQRSTTUVWXYZ&ctfffflffl
aaвbbcddeefgghijklmnop
qrrsтuvwxyz.,';:!?/·♀✠✱
1234567890
Speaking of earlier types, Goudy says:
The old fellows stole all of our best ideas.

Globe Gothic Bold, 1905
Drawn for American Type Founders at the suggestion of Joseph Phinney, the manager of its Boston branch, this was "the least satisfactory (to me) of all my types," Goudy said. There are other Globe Gothics in A.T.F. catalogues with which this should not be confused — if it matters.

DISTRUST
More Histo
Bold Displa

Goethe, 1932

Goethe was drawn for a specimen Goudy sent, at request of the organizing committee, to the Goethe Centenary Exhibition in Leipzig. "In the main," he said, it was "a lighter version, with slight changes and refinements, of Goudy Modern." Walter Tracy of English Monotype has found this face reminiscent of the late eighteenth-century Binny and Ronaldson type used by Daniel Berkeley Updike in *Printing Types: Their History, Form and Use.* His question is apt.[18]

A B C D E F G H I J K L M N O
P Q R S T U V W X Y Z & . , ' : ; ! ? -
a b c d e f g h i j k l m n o p q r s t u v w x
y z fi ff fl ffi ffl æ 1 2 3 4 5 6 7 8 9 0

Speaking of earlier types, Goudy says:
The old fellows stole all of our best ideas.

Goudy Bold Face [nc?], 1932

"Why I made it, I can't imagine," Goudy said. It is not the Goudy Bold issued by American Type Founders, for which Goudy had no responsibility.

**ABCEPNOTRmbdh
norspufvylg'-,.iaetc**

Goethe Italic, 1933

The companion type to Goethe. It was used in the Limited Editions Club's *Frankenstein,* where its eminent qualities as a book face are apparent.

A B C D E F G H I J K L M N O P
Q R S T U V W X Y Z & . , ' ; : ! ? -
a b c d e f g h i j k l m n o p q r s t u v w
x y z fi fl ff ffi Th ä ô 1 2 3 4 5 6 7 8 9 0

Speaking of earlier types, Goudy says :
The old fellows stole all of our best ideas.

Goudy Book [nc], 1933

See the remarks on Atlantis.

Goudy Antique, 1919

The date marks the beginning of the designs, which were first shown at the American Institute of Graphic Arts printing show in 1921. The matrices, the first Goudy cut himself, were finally engraved in 1926.

more by turning the leaves of the book of experience in their chosen trade than they would gain in the formal institutions established for that end. This is particularly true of the art of printing, as the elements of good expression and the thoughts of the best intellects are forced upon the minds of those who work at the composing-case. 1 2 3 4 5 6 7 8 9 0

ABCDEFGHIJKLMNOPQRSTVWXYZ&
abcdefghijklmnopqrstuvwxyzſtctfifflflffffi.,':;?!

Goudy Cursive, 1916

Goudy said this face was drawn at the suggestion of Clarence Marder (then of Marder, Luse and Company) and that it was "my own interpretation of early Roman cursive writing."

A B C D E F G H I J K L M
N O P Q R S T U V W X Y Z
a b c d e f g h i j k l m n o p q r s t u v w x y z
A J K N R QU Qu Th e g k m
n r v w x qu ct st fs . , ' ' ; : ! ? -
~ ~ $ 1 2 3 4 5 6 7 8 9 0 ~ ~

Speaking of earlier types, Goudy says:
The old fellows stole all of our best ideas.

Goudy Dutch [nc], 1927
The drawings were lost in the 1939 fire. The design was inspired by "some hand-writing on an envelope addressed to me by a correspondent in Holland. The script was so unusual in character that I immediately conceived the notion of making a type with it as a foundation."

Goudy Italic [nc], 1921?
Goudy drew the face to accompany Goudy Roman, but it never proceeded beyond drawings, which were destroyed in the 1939 fire.

Goudy Heavy Face, 1925
The story Goudy told was that Harvey Best, then the new president of the Lanston Monotype Company, wanted a heavy face and persuaded Goudy to design one. "As such a letter has little appeal to me I was slow in getting at it, but I finally did. I am quite certain that my design was more or less a disappointment to Best…."

ABCDEFGHIJKLMN
OPQRSTUVWXYZ&
abcdefghijklmnopqrs
tuvwxyzfifffffiflfflctst
.,';:!?-$1234567890
Speaking of earlier
types, Goudy says:

Goudy Lanston, 1912
Robert Hewitt of Ardsley, New York, commissioned Frederic Trevor Hill to write a book about Abraham Lincoln and asked Goudy to design a new type for it. Hewitt died before the book was set in type, and Goudy, who had not been paid, named the face Goudy Old Style and put it on the market. Later he designed a new face for American Type Founders and released the name Goudy Old Style to them for that type and renamed this one Goudy Antique. Many years later Lanston Monotype wanted to fit the type for the machine and, at Lanston's request, Goudy renamed it Goudy Lanston.

ABCDEFGHIJKLMNOP
QRSTUVWXYZ&.,';:!?-
abcdefghijklmnopqrstuvwx
yzfifffffiflfflctæœ$1234567890
Speaking of earlier types,

Goudy Heavy Face Italic, 1925
Companion face to the above.

ABCDEFGHIJKL
MMNOPPQRSTU
VUWXYZ&.,';:!?-
abcdefgghijklmno
pqrstuvwxyzfififfi
flffl$1234567890
Speaking of earlier
types, Goudy says:

Goudy Modern, 1918
See pages 101–3.

ABCDEFGHIJKLM
NOPQRSTUVWXY
Z&.,';:!?-fifflffiffl
abcdefghijklmnopqrs
tuvwxyz1234567890

Speaking of earlier types, Goudy says:
The old fellows stole all of our best ideas.

Goudy Modern Italic, 1919
See pages 101–3.

ABCDEFGHIJKLMN
OPQRSTUVWXYZ&
abcdefghijklmnopqrstuvwxyz
fiffffifl ffl 1234567890.,';:!?-
Speaking of earlier types, Goudy says:
The old fellows stole all of our best ideas.

Goudy Old Style Italic, 1916
See pages 99–101.

ABCDEFGGHIJJKL
MNOPQRST TUVW
XYYZ & fi ff ffi fl ffl ct Qu
abcdefghijklmnopqrstu
vwxyz.,';:!?-$1234567890
Speaking of earlier types,
Goudy says: The old fellows
stole all of our best ideas.

Goudy Newstyle, 1921
See pages 105–6.

ABCDEFGHIJKLMN
OPQRSTUVWXYZ&
abcdefghijklmnopqrst
uvwxyz ff fl ffl ct .,';:!?-
1234567890
Speaking of earlier types, Goudy says:
The old fellows stole all of our best ideas.

Goudy Open, 1918
Goudy said the face was suggested by the caption on a French engraving used as a frontispiece to Alfred Pollard's *Fine Books*. Walter Tracy has shrewdly suggested that the inspiration for going to such a source was the success of the Cochin type, issued by Lanston Monotype in 1916, adapted from the Cochin issued in Paris in 1912 by Deberny and Peignot, based on lettering in eighteenth-century French engravings. He also points out that there are only seventeen lower case letters and four capitals in the inscription in the Pollard book, so the rest of the Goudy face must have been his own.

ABCDEFGHIJKLM
NOPQRSTUVWXY
Z& .,';:!?- fi ff fl ffi ffl
abcdefghijklmnopqrs
tuvwxyz 1234567890

Goudy Old Style, 1915
See pages 99–101.

ABCDEFGHIJKLMN
OPQRSTUVWXYZ&
ABCDEFGHIJKLMNOPQRS
TUVWXYZ&fiff ffifl ffl .,';:!?-
abcdefghijklmnopqrst
uvwxyz$1234567890
Speaking of earlier types,
Goudy says: The old fellows

Goudy Open Italic, 1919
Here the relationship to Goudy Modern is reversed. Goudy designed the italic for Goudy Modern first and, to create this open italic, merely opened up that face.

ABCDEFGHIJKLMN
OPQRSTUVWXYYZ&
abcdefghijklmnoppq
rrstuvwxyz.,';:!?-G
fiffffifl ffl $1234567890
Speaking of earlier types,
Goudy says: The old fellows
stole all of our best ideas.

Goudy Roman, 1914

The date is for completion of the original drawings. Louis Orr of the Bartlett Press had asked for a new type. Goudy took his drawings to London to be cast by Caslon, but, because there were war rumors that summer and Caslon could not be sure of the future supplies of materials, it refused to make the type. Goudy then return-ed his fee to Orr. Later Barnhart Brothers and Spindler in Chicago cut trial matri-ces, which Goudy did not like. Finally, "when I was engraving matrices myself, I revamped the design, renaming the face Goudy Roman."

Homep Homep Ho
poem pope mop
mmmmmm ooooooo
eeeeeeeeeeee ppppp

Goudy Thirty, 1942

This type was made at the request of Lanston Monotype. It may strike sensibilities other than only mine as strange for the company to ask him to design a face that would be issued after his death, but that was the case, and that is how Lanston advertised it when it finally appeared after Goudy died. Presumably its name re-fers to the fact that Lanston had issued twenty-nine previous Goudy faces.

ABCDEFGHIJKLMNOPQRSTUV
WXYZ .,"´·:;!?fiflffffiffl &$1234567890
abcdefghijklmnopqrstuvwxyz

Goudy Stout, 1939

"In a moment of typographic weakness," Goudy wrote, "I attempted to produce a 'black' letter that would interest those advertisers who like the bizarre in their print." He cut only one size and no one asked for another.

ABCDEFG
HIJKLM
NOPQRST
UVWXYZ
G & ., -

Goudytype, 1916

The design was done for American Type Founders, for a type to be used where "a touch of quaintness" was wanted. "I was pleased with it at the time of its making," Goudy said, "for I felt it represented a liveliness of handling not hitherto express-ed in type… but that in itself was not enough to make it a good type."

ABCDEFGHIJKL
MNOPQRSTUVW
XYZabcdefghijklm
nopqrstuvwxyz$&
.:;,-!?'1234567890

Goudy Text, 1928

Ultimately, Goudy said, this black face was based on the Gutenberg forty-two-line Bible, via letters he had made for lines in *Typographica No. 5* and *Elements of Lettering*. "My drawings show a 'trait' on the lower-case b, h, k, l, which properly belong only to the 'l.' The 'trait' is a little pointed projection on the left side of the straight stem of the 'l' at the height of the lower-case 'middles' and (I think) was used to differentiate the 'l' from the figure one (1). In my ignorance I put a trait on the other straight ascending stems where it was not needed, a lapse I never expect to live down, although no one, as yet, has called me for it — praise be."

ABCDEFGHIJKLMN
OPQRSTUVWXYZ
abcdefghijklmnopqrstuvwxyz
&$ffl flfiffffi.:;-,'?!1234567890

Goudy Uncials [nc], 1927

The drawings, lost in the 1939 fire, were capitals based on the capitals of medieval scribes. Goudy had intended them to be used only as initials.

Hadriano Lower Case, 1930
Goudy said he did not want to design this face, but the Monotype company requested it. "I do not think anything ever came of it — praise be!"

Here are Letters mamemgh hmimmmpmrmsmtm Eggs Camera Fame Gist Merit it Ragime Dare Pirate Thirst Nights map parts sights are

Hasbrouck [nc], 1934
See Atlantis.

Hadriano Stone Cut, 1934
Strictly speaking, this face ought to be listed among those often attributed to Goudy but done by others. It is included here only because the original is in fact a Goudy type. For this one Sol Hess of Lanston Monotype simply made a white inline cut in Hadriano; Goudy said he liked it and so gave permission that it be issued as his.

ABCDEFGHIJ
KLMNOPQRS
TUVWXYZ&
1234567890.,'

Hebrew University [nc?], 1945
Goudy knew no Hebrew, but he was asked by the American Friends of the Hebrew University in Jerusalem to design a dedicated face for the institution. They supplied him with a German Hebrew face that had become a classic among European Jews plus a second that was widely used to print Hebrew texts in many countries as models.

Hadriano Title, 1918
The decision to design these pleasing and popular inscriptional capitals was a spur-of-the-moment one taken late one night and executed quickly. It is based on a rubbing of letters Goudy made form a Roman fragment in the Louvre in 1910 which had on it the name of the emperor Hadrian.

ABCDEFGHIJKLMN
OPQRSTUVWXYZ.·,
1234567890&

FWG SÁYS: THE OLD
FELLOWS STOLE ÁLL

Inscription Greek, 1928?
Actually, this is only eleven Greek capitals, those not copied by the Roman alphabet, made to be added to the eighteen-point Kennerley small capitals to form a Greek font.

ΦΙΛΗΣ ΤΟ ΛΑΜΠΡΟΝ ΚΑΙ ΣΟΦΟΝ
ΛΟΥΣ ΤΟ ΤΕΡΓΝΟΝ ΣΧΗΜΑΤΟΣ
ΔΩΝ Η ΒΛΗΖΟΥΣΑ.

Italian Old Style, 1924
See pages 106–9.

ABCDEFGHIJKLM
NOPQRSTUVWXY
Z&.,';:!?- fi ff ffi fl ffl ct st ℂ
abcdefghijklmnopqrs
tuvwxyz$1234567890

Speaking of earlier types,
Goudy says: The old fellows
stole all of our best ideas.

Kennerley Bold, 1924
See pages 97–99.

ABCDEFGHIJKLMNOPQ
RSTUVWXYZ& fi ff ffi fl ffl
abcdefghijklmnopqrstuvw
xyzctst.,';:!?-($1234567890

Speaking of earlier types,
Goudy says: The old fellows
stole all of our best ideas.

Italian Old Style Italic, 1924
See pages 106–9.

ABCCDEEFGHIJKLLM
NOPQQRSTCUVUWX
YZ&.,';:!?-fi fi ffi fl ffl ct st
abcdefghijklmnopqrs
tuvwxyz$1234567890

Speaking of earlier types,
Goudy says: The old fellows
stole all of our best ideas.

Kennerley Bold Italic, 1924
See pages 97–99.

ABCDEFGHIJKLMN
OPQRSTUVWXYZ&
abcdefghijklmnopqrstu
vwxyz.,';:!?-$1234567890

Speaking of earlier types,
Goudy says: The old fellows
stole all of our best ideas.

Kaatskill, 1929
This face was designed for the Limited Editions Club and first was used in its *Rip Van Winkle*. Goudy said, "It owes nothing in its design to any existing face, and the type therefore is as truly an American type as anything so hide-bound by tradition can be." However, it will bear comparison with Deepdene and even with a few other Goudy designs done in the late 1920s and early 30s. He may have meant only that it owed nothing to any existing type by anyone other than himself.

ABCDEFGHIJKLMNO
PQRSTUVWXYZ& ABCD
EFGHIJKLMNOPQRSTUVWXYZ&
abcdefghijklmnopqrst
uvwxyz ct fi ff ffi fl ffl .,';:!?-
1234567890

Kennerley Old Style, 1911
See pages 97–99.

ABCDEFGHIJKLMNOP
QRSTUVWXYZ&ÆŒℂℐ
abcdefghijklmnopqrstuvwxyz
æœfiffffifflffl ct st.,';:!?-$1234567890

Speaking of earlier types,
Goudy says: The old fellows
stole all of our best ideas.

Kennerley Old Style Italic, 1918
See pages 97–99.

ABCDEFGHIJKLMNO
PQRSTUVWXYZ&ÆŒ
abcdefghijklmnopqrstuvwxyz
æœfiffffiflffl.,';:!?-$1234567890

Lining gothic [nc], 1921
Drawings of this sans serif were completed, but when Robert Wiebking was late in cutting matrices the order for the type was canceled. It is a pity because the drawings had some qualities associated with Kabel and Futura, Goudy said, and it predated both of those faces.

PACK MY
BOX WITH

Kennerley Open Capitals, 1911
See pages 97–99.

ABCDEF
GHIJKLM
TUV&12

Lombardic Capitals, 1929
The Story of the Village Type gives 1921 as the date for the drawings and 1929 as the date for the cutting of the matrices. Goudy said, "I imagine the earlier date refers to the showing made in *Elements of Lettering* before the thought of cutting the design in type occurred to me. "Indeed, in the main they follow the Lombardic capitals shown in that book."

ABCDEFGHIJKL
MNOPQRSTUVW
XYZ

Klaxon, 1914
This face was made at the request of the advertising manager of Lovell, McConnell and Company of Newark, New Jersey, manufacturers of the automobile horn. Robert Wiebking cut matrices for three sizes, but they perished in the 1939 fire.

"A WARNING SIGNAL must not only waves on the drum of the ear, but it mind behind the ear and cause volitional signal should carry its alarm notice over the least one block, to even a deaf or slow-moving the wind and other noise of the street.

Marlborough, 1925
Named after Marlboro-on-Hudson, to which Goudy had moved two years earlier, this type has an intriguing history. Goudy had made nine-inch drawings for it, and only after a sixteen-point font was cut by Robert Wiebking did he notice that many features, especially the serifs, disappeared in the reduction. He later cut his own matrices for a redesigned version, but decided unfortunately not to make an effort to sell it. It was entirely destroyed in the 1939 fire.

ABCDEFGHIJKLMNOP
QRSTUVWXYZ&.,';:!?-
abcdefghijklmnopqrstuvwx
yzæœfiffffiflffl&$1234567890

Marlborough Text, 1944
Only the letters needed to print "Certificate of Honor" were cut. It was made for the International Printing Company.

Certificate of Honor Dgpsy

Millvale [nc], 1935
See Atlantis.

Mediaeval, 1930
See page 110.

ABCDEEFFGGHIJKLMN
OPQRSSTUVWXYZ&.,';:!?
abcdefghijklmnopqrstuvwxyz
fiffffiflffllllct æ œ $1234567890

Speaking of earlier types, Goudy says:
The old fellows stole all of our best ideas.

Monotype 38-E Roman, 1908
This face was made for Lanston Monotype for use in the original *Life* magazine. Since Goudy knew little about the Monotype machine at the time, the company made many changes in the letters to fit them. Goudy's judgment of the changes, done without his consultation, is a rare one for him: "Probably, however, they were as well done as I could have done them." Because the type was used so much by the Gimbel's department store in its advertising, it was known for years as Gimbel and also — "contrary to my wishes," said Goudy — as Goudy Old Style and Goudy Light.

ABCDEFGHIJKLM
NOPQRSTUVWXY
Z&ÆŒ.,';:!?-fiffffiflffl
abcdefghijklmnopqrstu
vwxyzæœ£$1234567890

Mercury [nc], 1933
See Atlantis.

Monotype 38-E Italic, 1908
Companion to the 38-E Roman.

ABCDEFGHIJKLM
NOPQRSTUVWXY
Z&ÆŒ.,';:!?-fiffffiflffl
abcdefghijklmnopqrstu
vwxyzæœ£$1234567890

Speaking of earlier types,

Mostert, 1932

Goudy had bought from Paul Hoeber, the medical book publisher, a handwritten book made by Annelise Mostert of Stuttgart in 1923. "The writing was well done, a pseudo-roman letter presenting an interesting page, and to recoup the cost of the book I used it as a basis for a type," he said. But the proofs displeased him, so he did not develop it further.

National Old Style, 1916

Known among printers for a couple of generations simply as National, this type was designed by Goudy at the request of Clarence Marder and made by American Type Founders. Marder had requested a type specifically made from Goudy's lettering for the National Biscuit Company fifteen years earlier. Goudy's judgment was, "As a display letter it probably compares favorably with many others we could do without."

ABCDEFGHIJKLMN
OPQRSTUVWXYZ&
abcdefghijklmnopqrs
tuvwxyzfiffflffiffl.,;':!?-$
1234567890

Murchison [nc], 1938

"I was asked by Mr. Murchison of the Photostat Corporation if I would see him regarding a new type for a composing machine he had invented," Goudy said. He then gave a very amusing description of this strange device. He designed a face and made matrices for the exact size needed, but it is obvious from his remarks that he disapproved entirely of it.

New Village Text, 1938

Goudy listed this as a separate face, but it is not, from his own evidence. The Grabhorns in San Francisco were planning a book on William Caxton and ordered Deepdene text for it. Casting about for something a little more distinctive, Goudy's son cast capitals of the twenty-four-point Tory Text to line with the lower case of the twenty-four-point Deepdene Text and Goudy gave the mongrel this name.

ABCDEFGHIJKLM
NOPQRSTUVWX
YZ& 1234567890
Cabcdefghijklmnopqr
stuvwxyzfflfffl «;:'!?.,'»

Nabisco, 1921

The National Biscuit Company asked Goudy for a dedicated face that would reflect drawn letters he had made for the company in 1901 or 1902 and it became the model for a type that was popular for a long time, known as National. Goudy said, however, he simply went ahead and designed a new type, without reference to his previous drawings.

ABCDEFGHIJKLMNOP
QRSTUVWXYZabcdef
ghijklmnopqrstuvwxyz
$&?!'-.:;,1234567890

Norman Capitals, 1910

These letters were designed for Norman T. A. Munder, formerly of the Munder-Thompson Company of Baltimore. Goudy had designed for him a catalogue for the George H. Merrill Company of Boston, makers of printers' ink. His original design was only for enough letters to print the company's name. At Munder's request he then designed the rest of the alphabet, and the type was made for Munder by American Type Founders.

ABCDEFGHIJKLMN
OPQRSTUVWXYZA

SEE THE QUICK
BROWN FOX JUMP

Ornate Title, 1931

Goudy must have been feeling nostalgic when he drew these odd capitals —having passed sixty-five and obviously feeling other people thought he was coming to his end. He said that "the letters I did for the Sunday School room [in Shelbyville, Illinois, in his youth] *may* be responsible for the idea of the face."

ABCDEFGHIJ
KLMNOPQRS
TUVWXYZ&.,''-
PRECIOUS

Pax [nc], 1936

The drawings were done and patterns cut, but Goudy was disappointed when he engraved matrices and saw the type. See also University of California Old Style.

Pabst Roman, 1902

Goudy's account of this type is straightforward: "Some lettering of advertisements for the Pabst Brewing Company, which I had done for the advertising manager, Joseph Kathrens, and placed through the J. Walter Thompson agency, attracted the attention of Mr. Powell, advertising manager for the department store of Schlesinger & Mayer. He asked if that particular lettering could be done into type. Drawings were made and delivered to him and paid for…. Powell later approached the American Type Founders Company, who cut a number of sizes."

ABCDEFGHIJKLM
NOPQRSTUVWX
YZabcdefghijklmnopqrst
uvwxyz *The and & of* ÆŒ
£$ff()-?.:;,!'1234567890

Powell, 1907

Mr. Powell was Goudy's first Kennerley, obviously. Five years after he had been midwife and more to the Pabst, he moved to the Mandel Brothers department store in Chicago and commissioned this type.

ABCDEFGHIJKLM
NOPQRSTUVW
XYZ&ÆŒ.,';:!?
abcdefghijklmno
pqrstuvwxyzæœ
fiffl$1234567890£

Pabst Italic, 1903

This was made to accompany the Pabst Roman Goudy had done the previous year.

ABCDEFGHIJKL
MNOPQRSTUV
WXYZabcdefghijklm
nopqrstuvwxyzABDG
MNPRTQu&$£ffff
ffffff?!';:-'.1234567890

Quinan Old Style [nc], 1932

Named for the editor of *The American Mercury*, who was looking for a new face for the magazine's heads. Goudy drew the letters for the magazine's consideration, but the design was rejected. The drawings perished in the 1939 fire.

ible to a high degree. In its essen
tial letter forms it presents few
departures from good tradition
although showing a new hand
ling of some features in indivi
THESE ARE THE CAPITALS
OF THE FONT. BDQFJG&

Record Title, 1927
Charles De Vinne, the grandson of American type designer Theodore Low De Vinne, requested this type for *The Architectural Record*, for the headings. It was displayed best in the May 1928 issue. Goudy said it was inspired by a treatise of Damianus Moyllus printed at Parma in 1480, which gave the geometrical proportions of an alphabet of roman capitals (this work has since become rather too well known to designers and typographers through the efforts of Stanley Morison).

IMP·CAESARI DIVI
NERVAE TRAIANO OPTI
ICO DACICO PONT MAX
IMP VII COS VIPP FORTISSIMO

Saks Goudy Bold, 1934
See pages 109–10.

ABCDEFGHIJKLMNO
PQRSTUVWXYZ&.,'-
FWG SAYS: THE OLD
FELLOWS STOLE ALL

Remington Typewriter, 1927
This whole project was ill advised from the beginning, although Goudy's study of the actions of the typewriter and its effect on the type the machine finally printed is very valuable. He said he never knew whether the face was used by Remington, since no one had ever written him a letter in it. Eventually, Lanston Monotype cast a type from the designs.

```
Dear Sir —
        See remingtn type de
interesting, made at Deepdene
is started. May yet master di
men and shame strangers, enter
demented mangy tramps and rip
stepsister may grasp this, a m
aiming at imaginary enterpris
```

Saks Goudy Italic, 1934
See pages 109–10.

ABCDEFGHIJKLMNOPQ
RSTUVWXYZ&.,';:!?-
abcdefghijklmnopqrstuvwxyz
ABCDEGPRT fi ff ffi fl ffl ft &
Speaking of earlier types, Goudy says:
The old fellows stole all of our best ideas.

Saks Goudy, 1934
See pages 109–10.

ABCDEFGHIJKLMNOP
QRSTUVWXYZ&.,';:!?-
ABCDEFGHIJKLMNOPQRSTUVWXYZ&
abcdefghijklmnopqrstuvw
xyz fi ff ffi fl ffl & 1234567890
Of earlier types, FWG says: The
old fellows stole our best ideas.

Sans Serif Heavy, 1929
This unhappy face was made for Lanston Monotype to compete with the new sans serifs coming into the United States from Germany and England. It disappointed Goudy as much as it did Lanston Monotype.

**ABCDEFGHIJKLMNOPQRSTUV
WXYZabcdefghijklmnopqrstuvw
xyz fi fl ff ffi ffl $1234567890 .,-':;!?&**
The alphabet is a system and series of symbols representing collectively the elements of written language; letters are the individual signs that compose the alphabet, each signifying primarily but one thing, what letter it is, i.e. its name. It does, however, have a secondary function, the part it plays

Sans Serif Light, 1930
Simply a lighter version of the heavy.

AAABCDEFGHIJKLMNOPQ
RRSSTTUVWXYZ&.,':;!?-
aabcdeɛfghijklmnopqrstu
vwxyzfiffffiflffl$1234567890

Speaking of earlier types,
Goudy says: The old fellows
stole all of our best ideas.

Scripps College Old Style Italic, 1944
Companion type to the Scripps College Old Style.

A B C Ç E F G H I L N O
P Q R S T U a b c d e f g
h i j l m n o p r s t u y ? , ;

Sans Serif Light Italic, 1931
This was made to accompany the Sans Serif Light, even though Goudy always preached that a sans serif face needs no italic.

AABCDEFGHIJKLMℳMNN
OPQRSTUVWXYZ&.,';:!?-
abcdefghijklmnopqrstuv
wxyzfiffffiflffl$1234567890

Speaking of earlier types,
Goudy·says: The old fellows
stole all of our best ideas.

Sherman, 1912
Goudy said this type was "one of my great disappointments." He designed it for Frederick Sherman, the publisher, who had Munder print *A Painter's Holiday* by Bliss Carmen in it. Goudy thought his drawings "really beautiful," but found the type, when cast, difficult to use. "I had at that time, due to inexperience, concluded that 'close fitting' of a type was a *sine qua non*, and in the Sherman type I went to extremes.... Where the type is now I do not know, as Sherman and I quarreled later over other business matters and I never saw him again."

FREDICSHAMNGT
pack my box with five
dzn lqur jgs 1234567
890 Qu& æ œ ct fl ffi
YQULVKJPZBWX, -

Scripps College Old Style, 1941
Dorothy Drake, the librarian of Scripps College in California, wanted type that students who were interested in book making could use. A donor gave a gift to Scripps to pay for it and Goudy's design was intended for use on a school press. He said it was straightforward but not foolproof.

ABCDEFGHIJKLMNOP
QRSTUVWXYZ&.,';:!?-
ABCDEFGHIJKLMNOPQRSTUVWXYZ&
abcdefghijklmnopqrstuvw
xyzfiffffiflfflctæct1234567890
Speaking of earlier types, Goudy

Spencer Old Style [nc?], 1943
A large book printing firm had commissioned its own face and Goudy had completed about fifty drawings when wartime restrictions on materials caused the company to cancel the order. Goudy completed the design as a gift for Syracuse University and named it for H. Lyle Spencer, dean of the university's School of Journalism.

phasg

Spencer Old Style Italic [nc?], 1943
Companion to Spencer Old Style.

Tory Text, 1935
Goudy was planning to print an edition of the medieval tale *Aucassin and Nicol-ette* and "the 'lettres batarde' shown in the Grolier Club edition of Geoffroy Tory's *Champ Fleury*… came to my mind." He said that in one of Tory's alphabets he found "exactly what I wanted." Tory Text is not, however, a copy of any of the Tory types.

ABCDEFGHIJKLMNOP
QRSTUVWXYZ&.,';:!?,
abcdefghijklmnopqrstuvwx
yz fi ff ffi fl ffl Th«»1234567890
Speaking of earlier types, Goudy says:
The old fellows stole all of our best ideas.

Strathmore Title [nc], 1929
This was made for Goudy's own convenience when he was designing a booklet for the Strathmore Paper Company about their "Old Strathmore" paper. He drew an entire alphabet of capitals, but cut only fourteen letters before he abandoned it.

STRATHMORE
OLD STRATFORD
BOOK PAPERS

Trajan Title, 1930
The face derives from an inscription at the base of Trajan's Column in Rome, which Goudy had seen twenty years earlier. He had made some letters based on it for the Limited Editions Club *Rip Van Winkle*. Later he was asked to design a capital font for a list of subscribers to the building of the Community House in Forest Hills Gardens, and he made the Trajan.

ABCDEFGHIJKLMNO
PQQRSTUVWXYZ&
1234567890.,'-
FWG SAYS THE OLD FELLOWS
STOLE ALL OF OUR BEST IDEAS

Textbook Old Style [nc], 1934
See Atlantis.

Truesdell, 1930
Goudy designed this face for *The Colophon* No. 5 and gave it his mother's maiden name. He claimed the capitals "follow more or less" the letters of early scribes.

ABCDEFGHIJKLMNOP
QRSTUVWXYZ&.,';:!?-
abcdefghijklmnopqrstu
vwxyz fi ff ffi fl ffl æ ct st (([
1234567890
Speaking of earlier types, Goudy says:
The old fellows stole all of our best

Truesdell Italic, 1930
Companion face to Truesdell.

A B C D E F G H I J K L M N O P
Q R S T U V W X Y Z & A B C
D E G K L P R T U V W Y Th ❧
a b c d e f g h i j k l m n o p q r s t u v
w x y z v y fi ff fl ffl ct st . , ' ; : ! ? -

Speaking of earlier types, Goudy says:
The old fellows stole all of our best ideas.

Unnamed [nc], 1896
The second set of drawings sent to the Dickinson Type Foundry, after it had issued Camelot. Goudy said it was slightly inclined but not a true italic. It was never cast.

University of California Old Style, 1938
When the director of the University of California Press asked Goudy for a proprietary face for the university, Goudy intended to give him the Pax type, which he had drawn, and for which he had cut almost all the master patterns, in 1936 or 1937. The origin of Pax is odd. At an Ulster-Irish Society dinner someone suggested Goudy make a type "that had something to do with peace." Anyway, he was disgusted with the proofs of that type and made the designs for University of California Old Style and cut the patterns at breakneck speed.

A B C D E F G H I J K L M N O
P Q R S T U V W X Y Z & . , '-: ; ! ?
ABCDEFGHIJKLMNOPQRSTUVWXYZ
a b c d e f g h i j k l m n o p q r s t u
v w x y z fi ff ffi fl ffl ct st Æ Œ æ œ
1 2 3 4 5 6 7 8 9 0

Unnamed [nc], 1917?
Goudy had zinc etchings made of this face and drew a proof from them. He decided the face was not good and it was not further developed. The drawings are in the Library of Congress.

PCK MY BX WITH
FV DZN JUGS LQR
quick brown fog day U
12 & l m j v z s fi x
BARDOE peath⸳ g

University of California Old Style Italic, 1938
Companion face to the Old Style. For the italic face Goudy did a number of swash capitals and a few for the lower case.

A B C D E F G H I J K L M N O P Q R S
T U V W X Y Z & Æ Œ æ ct st . , '- ; : ! ?
a b c d e f g h i j k l m n o p q r s t u v w x y z
fi ff fl ffi ffl A B C D E G M R T g v w

Speaking of earlier types, Goudy says:
The old fellows stole all of our best ideas.

Unnamed [nc], 1930?
One of two sets of unnamed designs destroyed in the 1939 fire. Goudy did not know how far along either was, but he had assigned them work numbers and so he assumed they were at least partly completed.

Unnamed [nc], 1930?
See previous entry.

Village No. 2, 1932
Goudy said that ever since Sherman bought the original Village type he had wanted to design another, making corrections of some features. The No. 2 he designed for a reprinting of Theodore L. DeVinne's *The Old and The New*. Lanston Monotype bought it and cut it in fourteen and eighteen point. But then there was a fight between Goudy and Lanston over some details of reproduction, so other sizes were not cut.

A B C D E F G H I J K L M N O P
Q R S T U V W X Y Z & A B C D E
F G H I J K L M N O P Q R S T U V W X Y Z
a b c d e f g h i j k l m n o p q r s t u v
w x y z fi ff ffi fl ffl 1 2 3 4 5 6 7 8 9 0
Speaking of earlier types, Goudy says :
The old fellows stole all of our best ideas.

Venezia Italic, 1925
This face was made at the request of the London designer and typographer George W. Jones, to accompany his Venezia roman. Stanley Morison said Goudy's face was based entirely on a French italic font cut by Claude Garamond around 1535. Goudy insisted, however, that he had made the design with reference only to Jones' roman.

De Præparatione Evangelica of Eusebius is generally considered Jenson's first book.

A B C D E F G H I J K L M N O P
Q R S T U V W X Y Z Æ Œ
a b c d e f g h i j k l m n o p q r s
t u v w x y z æ œ
1 2 3 4 5 6 7 8 9 0 £ , . : ; ' ' (-) ! ? &

Village Italic, 1934
Companion face to Village No. 2.

A B C D E F G H I J K L M N O P
Q R S T U V W X Y Z & a b c d e f g
h i j k l m n o p q r s t u v w x y z ct st ff ffl
Speaking of earlier types, Goudy says :
The old fellows stole all of our best ideas.

Village, 1903
Originally designed for the Kuppenheimer clothing firm, which then decided it would be too expensive to make, the face was based, Goudy said, on "the types of Jenson, as exhibited in Morris' Golden type, the Doves, Montaigne, Merrymount, and types of that ilk." That is a very large ilk. The matrices became the property of Frederick Sherman eventually.

❦IT WAS THE TERRACE OF
God's house
That she was standing on, —
By God built over the sheer depth
In which Space is begun;
So high, that looking downward

IGb

rætl Bis

O

NOTES

1. This and the following remarks by Horace Hart, Herbert Johnson, Alexander Lawson, and Robert Leslie come from interviews or telephone conversations with the author in 1986–87.

2. Joseph Blumenthal, *The Printed Book in America* (Boston: David R. Godine, 1977).

3. Peter Bielenson, *The Story of Frederic W. Goudy* (Philadelphia: The Lanston Monotype Machine Company [Printed for The Distaff Side], 1939).

4. Telephone conversation with the author, January 1987.

5. Unless otherwise noted, the material in this chapter is drawn from Goudy's *Typologia* (Berkeley and Los Angeles: University of California Press, 1940) and *The Alphabet and Elements of Lettering* (New York: Dover Publications, 1963). A reading of all the Goudy speeches in the collection of the Library of Congress will reveal what Goudy himself said, that he used his previous pronouncements to write *Typologia* and even quoted verbatim large sections of his own writing (especially from *Ars Typographica*) in that book.

6. Frederic W. Goudy, *Type Revivals* (Lexington, Va.: Journalism Laboratory Press, Washington and Lee University, 1937).

7. The details of Goudy's life and most of the things said by or about him as set forth in this chapter are drawn from the books listed below; magazine and newspaper articles, notes, and letters in the Frederic and Bertha Goudy Collection, Library of Congress, Washington, D.C., and the Melbert B. Cary Collection of Goudyana, Grolier Club Library, New York; and unpublished typescripts in the Melbert B. Cary Graphic Arts Collection, Rochester Institute of Technology, New York. A very few details are drawn from interviews with people who remember Goudy and who are listed in the acknowledgments. Most of the information and the quotations, unless otherwise acknowledged, come from the following books: Bielenson, *Story of Goudy*; Melbert B. Cary, Jr., *A Bibliography of the Village Press* (New York: The Press of the Woolly Whale, 1938); Bertha S. Goudy, *First Lady of Printing: Remembrances of the Distaff Side of the Village Press* (New York: The Distaff Side, 1958); Frederic W. Goudy, *Bertha M. Goudy: Recollections by One Who Knew Her Best* (Marlboro-on-Hudson, N.Y.: The Village Press, 1939); Frederic W. Goudy, *A Half-Century of Type Design and Typography, 1895–1945* (New York: The Typophiles, 1946); *Frederic William Goudy, Art Director to the Lanston Monotype Company, 1920–1939, Typographic Counsel, 1939–1947* (Philadelphia: The Lanston Monotype Machine Company, 1947); [Mitchell Kennerley, Charles E. Park, and Will Ransom], *Intimate Recollections of The Village Press by Three Friends* (Marlborough, N.Y.: The Village Press, 1938); Vrest Orton, *Goudy: Master of Letters* (Chicago: The Black Cat Press, 1939); *The Village Press, A Retrospective Exhibition 1903–1933* (New York: The American Institute of Graphic Arts, 1933).

8. Orton, *Goudy: Master of Letters*.

9. The book is in the Grolier Club Library.

10. The account is in an undated, unsigned typescript in the Cary Goudyana collection in the Grolier Club Library.

11. See David McKitterick, editor, *Stanley Morison and D. B. Updike: Selected Correspondence* (London: The Scolar Press, 1972).

12. *In Reply: An Open Letter to Frederic W. Goudy From Bruce Rogers Done for the Celebration of the Thirty-fifth Anniversary of The Village Press, July Twenty-third, 1938* (New York: Printed by Earl H. Emmons, 1938).

13. *Son of a Goudy. An Open Letter to Frederic W. Goudy From His Nearest Kin and Severest Critic Fred T. Goudy, Done for the Thirty-fifth Anniversary of The Village Press Celebrated July Twenty-third, 1938* (New York: The Maverick Press, 1938).

14. Unpublished typescript of a life of Goudy by Howard Coggeshall in the Cary collection, Rochester Institute of Technology.

15. Arthur Rushmore to Paul Bennett [?], May 13, 1947, Goudy collection, Library of Congress.

16. The Hart volume is extremely rare now. But there are several volumes on types that illustrate not only the Fell, but virtually every important typeface. The best by far is Stanley Morison's *Four Centuries of Fine Printing — Upwards of Six Hundred Examples of the Works of Presses Established During the Years 1500 to 1922* (London: Ernest Benn Ltd., 1924). It is not as rare as the Hart, but, unfortunately, can be found in only a small number of libraries. More accessible is *The Typographic Book, 1450–1935* by Morison and Kenneth Day (Chicago: University of Chicago Press, 1963). *Printing Types — Their History, Forms and Use: A Study in Survivals* by Daniel Berkeley Updike (Cambridge, Mass.: Harvard University Press, 1937) is a very good reference, but not all its illustrations are extensive enough to give one a whole alphabet. There are many other volumes of reproductions of old types, several by Morison and many more recent ones. The problem with the recent publications is that most are printed in offset rather than letterpress and will not give a reader a chance to judge the impression of the type.

17. See Robert D. Harban, *Chapter Nine* (New York: The Typophiles, 1982).

18. Walter Tracy, *Letters of Credit: A View of Type Design* (Boston: David R. Godine, 1986).

18. Walter Tracy, *Letters of Credit: A View of Type Design* (Boston: David R. Godine, 1986).

INDEX

Illustrations and samples of typefaces are indicated with *italic* figures.

Advertisers' Modern, *118*
Advertisers' Roman, *118*
advertising, Goudy's work in, 44–51, 76, 87, 109
Alden, Richard Coe, 43–4
The Alphabet and *Elements of Lettering*, *26–8, 27–8*, 32, *34*, 56, 59, *78–81, 78*
American Cat News, 50, 50
American Institute of Architecture, Gold Medal, 60
American Institute of Graphic Arts, 84, 101, 110
  Gold Medal, 60, 112
Amherst Club, dinner, 1939, *61*
Aries, 110, *118*, 123
Ars Typographica, 27, 56, 59, 74, 82, *85*, 115
Art Nouveau, 109
Art Students' League, Manhattan, 56
Ashbee, C. R., 38, 39
Atlantis, 119, 124, 129, 131, 136
Auditorium Theater, Chicago, *43*

Baskerville, 31–2, 55
Bauhaus, 17
Bayer, Herbert, Universal lowercase only, *37*
Beardsley, Aubrey, 45, 98
Bennett, Paul, *53*
Benton, Morris, 31, 98, 101
Bertham, *68*, 71, *72, 119*
Bielenson, Peter, 63
Blumenthal, Joseph, 15
Bodoni, 31–2, 99, 109
Booklet Old Style, *119*
Booklet Press, 44
Bradley, Will, 44, 45, 82
Bridges, Robert, 105–6
Bullen, Henry Lewis, 60, 98, 99
Bulmer, William, 84

Cambridge City Bakery, ad for, *48*
Camelot, 45, *119*, 137
Camelot Press, ad for, *45*, 45
Caslon, 31–2, 55
Caxton, William, 45, 132
Caxton Initials, *120*
Champ Fleury, 109, 110
The Chap-Book, 44–5, *45*, 82
Chicago, as design center in the 1890s, 42–4, 49
classicism, Goudy's definition, 32
Cloister Initials, *120*
Cobden-Sanderson, Charles James, 44, 97–8
Coggeshall, Howard, *61*, 67, 72
Collier Old Style, 56, *120*
Columbian Exposition, Chicago, 1893, *42*, 42
Companion Old Style, *120*
Copperplate Gothic, *121*
Crane, Stephen, 45
Curtis Publishing Co., booklet for, *49*
Cushing Italic, *121*

De evangelica praeparatione, *30*
De Vinne Roman, 45, *122*
Deepdene (house and mill), Marlboro-on-Hudson:
  fire, 71–2
  Goudy's workshop, *62–3*
  house, *63, 66*
  mill, *64–5*
  move to, 65
Deepdene Rd., Queens, move to, 56
Deepdene typefaces, 18, *20–1*, 22–5, 65, 115, *121–2*, 128, 132
  lowercase, *19, 22–5*
  uppercase, *24–5*
design:
  Bauhaus, 17
  Deepdene salon, 56
  in the 1890s, 42–3
  good, Goudy on, 31–3, 36–8, 95
  in Hingham, 51

standards of, 93, 95
The Door in the Wall and Other Stories, 55, 56, *74–5*, 76, 78
Dürer, Albrecht, 27
Dwiggins, Mabel, 51, 53, 67
Dwiggins, W. A., 51, 74, 84, 88

Emmons, Earl, 68, 72
Endeavor type, *39*
Everson, William, 103

Fables in Spring, 50
Fleuron, 59, 62, 101
Forum Title, 55, 115, *123*
France, Anatole, 45
Franciscan, *96, 110–11*, 110, 118, *123*
Futura, 130

Garamond, 61, 84, *104*
Garamond, Claude, 31–2, 59, 103
Garamont, 59, 61, 96, 103, *105*, 105, *123*
Gimbel, 131
Globe Gothic Bold, *123*
Goethe, 65, 103, 115, *124*
Golden, *39*, 50, 101, 138
Good King Wenceslas, 53, *111*
Goudy, Alice, 66, 68
Goudy, Bertha, 44, 45, 48, 51, 53, *54*, 54–5, 63, 65, *66*, 66–8, *69*, 71, 72, 78, 84
Goudy, Frederic T., 48, 66–7, *67*, 132
Goudy, Frederic W., *14, 16, 17, 24, 28–9, 40–1, 52–4*, 56, *60–1, 63, 66–7, 73, 88–90, 92–3*, 95, 113–15
  life of, 41–73
Goudy Antique, 120, *124*, 125
Goudy Bible, 106
Goudy Bold Face, *124*
Goudy Book, 124
Goudy Cursive, *124*
Goudy Dutch, 125
"The Goudy Family," *101*
Goudy Friar, *72, 94, 95, 123*
Goudy Heavy Face, *125*
Goudy Italic, 125

Goudy Lanston, 56, *125*
Goudy Light, 54, 131
Goudy Modern, 18, 56, *96*, 101, *102, 103*, 103, 124, *125, 126*
Goudy Newstyle, 18, 59, *72*, 82, *96*, 105–6, *106*, 115, *126*
Goudy Old Style, 54, 56, 60, *96*, 99, *100, 101*, 101, 125, *126*, 131
Goudy Open, 56, 103, *126*
Goudy Roman, *127*
Goudy Stout, *127*
Goudy Text, 65, 115, *127*
Goudy Thirty, 59, *127*
Goudy Tory, *72*, 132
Goudy Uncials, 127
Goudytype, *127*
Grabhorn, Edwin, 72, 106, 110, 123
"Granite and Cypress," 101, *102*

Hadriano, 55, *129*
A Half-Century of Type Design and Typography, 71, 72, 106, 117, 118
Hammer, Victor, 123
Hart, Horace, 16
Hasbrouk, 129
"Hearst" type, 49, 71
Hebrew University, 66, *129*
Heger, Frank, 114
Hingham, Massachusetts, 67
  move to, 51
Holbein, Hans, 99
Holme, Frank, 49, 50
Hoyem, Andrew, 25

initials, drawings of, *48, 74*, 127
The Inland Printer, 44, *46–7*, 84, *86*
"An Innovation in Letter Founding," 59
Inscription Greek, *128*
Italian Old Style, 18, 59–60, *96*, 106, *107–8*, 109, 115, *128*

Jannon, Jean, 59

Janson, 99
Jaugeon, projection of capitals onto squares, *37*, 38
Jenson, Nicolaus, 18, 30, 31, 33, 50, 59, 98–9, 109
Goudy's drawings of Jenson's work, *31*
Johnson, Herbert, 16
Johnson, John, 54
Johnston, Edward, 18
Jones, George W., *54*, 54, 112, 115
Junior Advertising Club, Los Angeles, 1939, *60*

Kaatskill, *72*, *128*
Kabel, 130
Kelmscott Press, 44
Kennerley, 55, *75*, 78, *96*, 97–9, *98–100*, 101, *128*, 129, *130*
Kennerley, Mitchell, *52*, 53–5, 60, 75, 76, 84
King's fount, *39*
Klaxon, 103, *116–17*, *130*
Koch, Rudolf, 88, 90–2, 123

Lanston Monotype, 59, 91, 105
Lawson, Alexander, 16
"Le Bonheur de ce monde," 77, 78
legibility, Goudy on, 36–8
Leslie, Dr. Robert, 16
Library of Congress, Goudy collection, 71, 72, 87
Lining Gothic, *130*
Lombardic Capitals, *130*
"Lost Goudy Types," *72*
Lowe, Cyril, 56
Lozier, Lewis Hogarth, 50
Lutetia, 23, 106

machines, Goudy on, 95
Marlborough, 115, *130*
Marlborough Text, *131*
Mediaeval, *72*, *96*, *110*, 110, *131*
Mercury, 131
Meynell, Sir Francis, 101, 115, 123
Millard, George, 44

Millvale, 131
modern, type classification, defined, 22
Modern Advertising, 44, *44*
Monotype, 38-E, 54, *131*
Morison, Stanley, 27, 39, 55, 59, 61–2, 88, 90, 97, 101, 103
Morris, May, *42*
Morris, William, 16, 31, 38, 39, *42*, 42, 44, 50, 51, 54, 55, 76, 90, 91, 97, 101, 138
Mosher, Thomas B., 48
Mostert, 132
Motteroz, *39*
Moxon, Joseph, 27–8
Murchison, 132

Nabisco, *132*
Nadal, Berne, 45
National, 132
New Village Text, *132*
Newberry Library, 44
Norman Capitals, *132*
A Note on Letter-Design and the Village Types, 82
Notes on a Century of Typography at the University Press, Oxford, 98

old style, defined, 22
originality, Goudy on, 31, 50
Ornate Title, *133*
orthography, English, 105
Orton, Vrest, 41, 42

Pabst, 49–50, *133*
Park, Charles, 51
Pax, *133*, 137
Peerless Motor Co., ad for, *87*
Plantin, Christoph, 76–8, 84
Pollard, Alfred W., 54
Pont, Charles E., 65, 114
Powell, *133*
Printing, 51
printing, good, Goudy's rules for, 38, 59, 95

Quinan Old Style, *133*

Ransom, Will, 28, 51, 67

Rasselas, 36
readability, Goudy on, 36–8
Record Title, 134
Remington Typewriter, 65–6, 91, *134*
Ricketts, Sir Charles W., 38, 39, 44, 45, 55, 84, 97
Rogers, Bruce, 16, 23, 31, 49, 50, *53*, 53, 60, 61, 63, 67, 74, 84, 88, 106, 109, 111, 123
Root, Robert, 41, 42
Rudge, William Edwin, 23, 56
Rusher, Phillip, 36, 38
Rushmore, Arthur, 72
Ruskin, John, 16, 42

Saints and Sinners Corner, 44
"Saks *Fifth Avenue*," 109
Saks-Goudy, *96*, *109*, 109–10, *134*
Sans Serif Heavy, *134*
Sans Serif Light, *135*
School of Illustration, Chicago, 49–51
Scripps College Old Style, *135*
Sherman, 135
The Songs and Poems of Sir John Suckling, 44
Songs and Verses Selected from the Works of Edmund Waller, Esq., 76, 78
Spencer Old Style, *135*, 136
Sprinks, Bertha Matilda, *see* Goudy, Bertha
Stern, Alexander, 112
Stone, Herbert S., 44, 50
The Story of the Glittering Plain, 43
Strathmore Title, *136*
style, defined, 38
Sullivan, Louis, 42–3

T & T Imprint, 87
Textbook Old Style, *136*
Thomas, Lowell, 68
Times Roman, 39
Tory, Geoffroy, 27, 109, 110
Tory Text, 110, *136*
Toulouse-Lautrec, Henri de, 45
Tracy, Walter, 23, 124

tradition, Goudy on, 31–3
Trajan Title, *34*, 65, *72*, 136
Trajan's Column, Rome, *34–5*, 55, 123, 136
Trattato di scientia d'arme, 22
"A Tribute to B.M.G.," *68*
Truesdell, *136*, *137*
type, digitized, standards of design, 95
"The Type Speaks," *23*, 68, 71
Typographica, 57–9, 59, 82, *84*, *99*, *103*, *105*, *106*, 127
typography, good, Goudy's rules for, 38, 95
Typologia, 28, 36, 38, *70*, 71, 72, 81, *82–3*, 91–3
Typophiles, 16, 72, 117

University of California Old Style, *70*, 71, 81, 87, 133, *137*
Updike, Daniel Berkeley, 39, 53, 61–2, 68, 88–90, 99, 103, 124

Vale, *39*, 44, 101
Venezia Italic, 115, *138*
Verlaine, Paul, 45
Vest Pocket series, 48
Village, *138*
Village Letter Foundery, 56, 59
Village No. 2, 65, *72*, *138*
Village Press, 16, 28, 50, 51, 53, 55, 62, 65–8, 78, 82, 117
fires, 54, 71–2, 117–19, 125, 127, 129, 131, 136–8
move to Manhattan, 53
printer's mark, *51*
Vox, Maximilian, 22

Walker, Sir Emery, *42*, *54*, 54, 110
Welles, Clara Barck, 42
Wells, H. G., 45, 55
Wiebking, Robert, 63
Wright, Frank Lloyd, 42

Zenner, Alfred, 45, 48
Zenner Disinfectant Co., ad for, *49*

DOCUMENTS OF AMERICAN DESIGN

Documents of American Design is a nonprofit corporation established in 1984 by a group of graphic designers, art directors, and educators to assess and preserve the record of American graphic design. Its projects include exhibitions, seminars, and books, of which *Frederic Goudy* is the second book in the Masters of American Design series. The first was *Brodovitch* by Andy Grundberg.

These undertakings are intended to inform professional and general audiences and to further the knowledge of the history and role of graphic design in our culture. Future projects will include Saul Bass, Will Burtin, and Will Bradley.

Documents of American Design is deeply indebted to many individuals and organizations for their help and support. This book and the books that follow could not happen without their advice and contributions. We are very grateful to them.

Our benefactors include Aaron Burns and the International Typeface Corporation, The Cooper Union for the Advancement of Science and Art, Cowles Charitable Trust, Jean Coyne and Richard Coyne of *Communication Arts* magazine, Carl Fischer, Alvin Grossman, Kit Hinrichs, Neil Shakery, and Linda Hinrichs of Pentagram, Ken Lieberman of Ken Lieberman Labs, The National Endowment for the Arts, and James Stockton of James Stockton & Associates.

Contributors to the development of *Documents of American Design* and this book include Jennifer Antupit, Mary K. Baumann, Barbara Berger, Kathy Corrigan, Dan Erkkila, Annie Fink, Patricia Galteri of Meyer, Souzzi, English, and Klein, Alan Green, David L. Green, Amy K. Hughes, Bill N. Lacy, Joseph Lee, David Matava, Susan B. Moore, Peg Patterson and Tom Wood of Patterson and Wood, Judith Rew, Michael Saridis, Debora K. Schuler, Arthur Tarlow, and Phyllis Wender of Rosenstone-Wender.

For their help in preparing *Frederic Goudy* for publication, we would like to thank Norman Cordes of Cordes Printing, Inc., Linda Eger, Pat Taylor of Out of Sorts Letter Foundery, and the Hiram Halle Memorial Library, Pound Ridge, New York.

While every attempt has been made to include proper and accurate credits for our sponsors and for all work appearing in this book, we apologize for any oversights. Errors will be corrected in future editions.

CREDITS

Fine printin
type withou
one that is easi
ly readable, masculi
and not made to display

but instead to help the reader. Type must be easy to read, graceful, but not weak; decorative, but not ornate; beautiful in itself and in composition; austere and formal, with no stale or uninteresting regularity in its irregular parts; simple in design, but not with the bastard simplicity of form which is mere crudity of